Religion in America

RELIGION IN AMERICA

ORIGINAL ESSAYS ON RELIGION IN A FREE SOCIETY

1368

edited by John Cogley

Meridian Books
THE WORLD PUBLISHING COMPANY
Cleveland and New York

The essays in this volume are based on papers delivered at a Seminar on Religion in a Free Society sponsored by The Fund for the Republic, Inc. The Seminar was held at the World Affairs Center in New York from May 5 to May 9, 1958.

John Cogley, editor of the volume, serves as Staff Administrator for the Fund's project on Religion in a Free Society.

AN ORIGINAL MERIDIAN BOOK

Published by The World Publishing Company
2231 West 110th Street, Cleveland 2, Ohio
First printing September 1958
Sixth printing June 1963
Library of Congress Catalog Card Number: 58-12381
Printed in the United States of America   6wp663

CONTENTS

INTRODUCTION

PART V: RELIGION AND THE FREE SOCIETY

NOTES ON CONTRIBUTORS

INTRODUCTION

Something exciting happens when intelligent people get together to talk intelligently about important matters. It happened recently at a seminar on Religion in a Free Society which was sponsored by the Fund for the Republic. Early in May, 1958, a group of about a hundred persons gathered for almost a week at the World Affairs Center in New York. They came together in order to talk candidly about a number of matters that are too often whispered about behind locked sectarian doors. Individually, they represented Protestantism, Catholicism, Judaism and various shades of non-belief, but they came together as fellow citizens who share a common concern for the free society of America.

Among them were lawyers, professors, clergymen of all faiths, journalists, educators and a variety of publicists. To no one's surprise, they discovered after almost a week of discussion that they disagreed, and probably always would, about some of the things that matter most in life. But they also discovered that they agreed much more than they thought they did about certain other things, and this was a pleasant surprise for some of them. Moreover, they discovered that they liked each other. When they broke up to return to their homes, it was with a certain measure of regret that they would not be seeing more of each other in the future.

One participant said he believed that none of them would ever be quite the same again. That might have been an exaggeration, but certainly for these people, some of whom had been engaged in bitter religious controversy with each other for many years, the "enemy" now had a face and it was a face not very different from anyone else's. Some of them, I suspect, *listened* for the first time in years. They listened to the other fellow's side of the argument and heard someone else present their own.

The seminar, in the high enthusiasm of its closing hours, was described as historic. That, too, is probably an exaggeration, but it is just possible that during those five days understanding among Americans of different belief, and the continuing debate about which the Founding Fathers spoke, were helped along a little. Perhaps the Civilization of the Dialogue came just a bit closer to being a reality. Most of those who attended the seminar thought so. One of them said that he had learned a big lesson; he had learned that the free society of America means more than an agreement to disagree; it is posited, rather, on the idea that Americans will disagree in order to agree.

The main reason why the seminar did not freeze into the unbending hostility that would have made conversation impossible or, what would have been worse, melt into the sweet nothingness that would have made conversation meaningless, was because the main speakers did not let it happen. They struck just the right note in their presentations. They were forthright without being impertinent. They were pertinent without being parochial. They were authoritative without being authoritarian. Most of all, they were thoughtful. They were chosen because they were known to be the kind of men who do not fritter away their time either on sectarian special-pleading or whoozy generalities. They were chosen because it was known that they were the kind of men who find something important to say when they agree to speak on important matters. Religion and the Free Society is an important topic, and, out of their separate traditions, they all found something stimulating to say about it. They disagreed strongly among themselves. On several questions they took diametrically opposed positions. They gave their audience something to think about and something to talk about. They lifted the level of some old debates to new heights. Several of them, indeed, had an electrifying effect on all who heard them.

It is in the hope that the lightning will strike twice that these essays, based on the talks given at the seminar, have been brought together between covers for a wider audience.

JOHN COGLEY

PART I: *Religious Pluralism and Civic Unity*

1

AMERICA'S FOUR CONSPIRACIES

John Courtney Murray

I

The "free society" seems to be a phrase of American coinage. At least it has no comparable currency in any other language, ancient or modern. The same is true of the phrase "free government." This fact of itself suggests the assumption that American society and its form of government are a unique historical realization. The assumption is generally regarded among us as unquestionable.

However, we have tended of late to pronounce the phrase, "the free society," with a rising interrogatory inflection. The phrase itself, it seems, now formulates a problem. This is an interesting new development. It was once assumed that the American proposition, both social and political, was self-evident; that it authenticated itself on simple inspection; that it was, in consequence, intuitively grasped and generally understood by the American people. This assumption now stands under severe question.

What is the free society, in its "idea"? Is this "idea" being successfully realized in the institutions that presently determine the pattern of American life, social and personal? The web of American institutions has altered, rapidly and profoundly, even radically, over the past few generations. Has the "idea" of the free society perhaps been strangled by the tightening intricacies of the newly formed institutional network? Has some new and alien "idea" subtly and unsuspectedly assumed the role of an organizing force in American society? Do we understand not only the superficial facts of change in American life but also the underlying factors of change—those "variable constants" that forever provide the dynamisms of change in all human life?

The very fact that these questions are being asked makes it sharply urgent that they be answered. What is at stake is America's understanding of itself. Self-understanding is the necessary condition of a sense of self-identity and self-confidence, whether in the case of an individual or in the case of a people. If the American people can no longer base this sense on naive assumptions of self-evidence, it is imperative that they find other more reasoned grounds for their essential affirmation that they are uniquely a people, uniquely a free society. Otherwise the peril is great. The complete loss of one's identity is, with all propriety of theological definition, hell. In diminished forms it is insanity. And it would not be well for the American giant to go lumbering about the world today, lost and mad.

At this juncture I suggest that the immediate question is not whether the free society is really free. This question may be unanswerable; it may even be meaningless as a question, if only for the reason that the norms of freedom seem to have got lost in a welter of confused controversy. Therefore I suggest that the immediate question is whether American society is properly civil. This question is intelligible and answerable, because the basic standard of civility is not in doubt: "Civilization is formed by men locked together in argument. From this dialogue the community becomes a political community." [1] This statement exactly expresses the mind of St. Thomas Aquinas, who was himself giving refined expression to the tradition of classic antiquity, which in its prior turn had given first elaboration to the concept of the "civil multitude," the multitude that is not a mass or a herd or a huddle, because it is characterized by civility.

The specifying note of political association is its rational deliberative quality, its dependence for its permanent cohesiveness on argument among men. In this it differs from all other forms of association found on earth. The animal kingdom is held together simply by the material homogeneity of the species; all its unities and antagonisms are of the organic and biological order. Wolves do not argue the merits of running in packs. The primal

[1] Thomas Gilby, O.P., *Between Community and Society*, London, Longmans Green, 1953, p. 93.

human community, the family, has its own distinctive bonds of union. Husband and wife are not drawn into the marital association simply by the forces of reason but by the forces of life itself, importantly including the mysterious dynamisms of sex. Their association is indeed founded on a contract, which must be a rational and free act. But the substance and finality of the contract is both infra- and supra-rational; it is an engagement to become "two in one flesh." The marital relationship may at times be quarrelsome, but it is not argumentative. Similarly, the union of parents and children is not based on reason, justice, or power; it is based on kinship, love, and *pietas.*

It is otherwise with the political community. I am not, of course, maintaining that civil society is a purely rational form of association. We no longer believe, with Locke or Hobbes, that man escapes from a mythical "state of nature" by an act of will, by a social contract. Civil society is a need of human nature before it becomes the object of human choice. Moreover, every particular society is a creature of the soil; it springs from the physical soil of earth and from the more formative soil of history. Its existence is sustained by loyalties that are not logical; its ideals are expressed in legends that go beyond the facts and are for that reason vehicles of truth; its cohesiveness depends in no small part on the materialisms of property and interest. Though all this is true, nevertheless the distinctive bond of the civil multitude is reason, or more exactly, that exercise of reason which is argument.

Hence the climate of the City is likewise distinctive. It is not feral or familial but forensic. It is not hot and humid, like the climate of the animal kingdom. It lacks the cordial warmth of love and unreasoning loyalty that pervades the family. It is cool and dry, with the coolness and dryness that characterize good argument among informed and responsible men. Civic amity gives to this climate its vital quality. This form of friendship is a special kind of moral virtue, a thing of reason and intelligence, laboriously cultivated by the discipline of passion, prejudice, and narrow self-interest. It is the sentiment proper to the City. It has nothing to do with the cleavage of a David to a Jonathan, or with the kinship of the clan, or with the charity, *fortis ut mors,* that makes the solidarity of the Church. It is in direct contrast with the passionate fanaticism of the Jacobin: "Be my brother or I'll kill you!" Ideally, I suppose, there should be only one passion in the city—the passion for justice. But the will to justice, though it engages the heart, finds its measure as it finds its origin in intelligence, in a clear understanding of what is due to the equal citizen from the City and to the City from the citizenry according to the mode of their equality. This commonly shared will to justice is the ground of civic amity as it is also the ground of that unity which is called peace.

This unity, qualified by amity, is the highest good of the civil multitude and the perfection of its civility.

If then society is civil when it is formed by men locked together in argument, the question rises, what is the argument about? There are three major themes.

First, the argument is about public affairs, the *res publica*, those matters which are for the advantage of the public (in the phrase as old as Plato) and which call for public decision and action by government. These affairs have their origin in matters of fact; but their rational discussion calls for the Socratic dialogue, the close and easy use of the habit of cross-examination, that transforms brute facts into arguable issues.

Second, the public argument concerns the affairs of the commonwealth. This is a wider concept. It denotes the affairs that fall, at least in decisive part, beyond the limited scope of government. These affairs are not to be settled by law, though law may be in some degree relevant to their settlement. They go beyond the necessities of the public order as such; they bear upon the quality of the common life. The great "affair" of the commonwealth is, of course, education. It includes three general areas of common interest: the school system, its mode of organization, its curricular content, and the level of learning among its teachers; the later education of the citizen in the liberal art of citizenship; and the more general enterprise of the advancement of knowledge by research.

The third theme of public argument is the most important and the most difficult. It concerns the constitutional consensus whereby the people acquires its identity as a people and the society is endowed with its vital form, its entelechy, its sense of purpose as a collectivity organized for action in history. The idea of consensus has been classic since the Stoics and Cicero; through St. Augustine it found its way into the liberal tradition of the West: *"Res publica, res populi; populus autem non omnis hominum coetus quoquo modo congregatus, sed coetus multitudinis iuris consensu et utilitatis communione sociatus"* (Scipio).

The state of civility supposes a consensus that is constitutional, *sc.*, its focus is the idea of law, as surrounded by the whole constellation of ideas that are related to the *ratio iuris* as its premises, its constituent elements, and its consequences. This consensus is come to by the people; they become a people by coming to it. They do not come to it accidentally, without quite knowing how, but deliberatively, by the methods of reason reflecting on experience. The consensus is not a structure of secondary rationalizations erected on psychological data (as the behaviorist would have it) or on economic data (as the Marxist would have it). It is not the residual minimum left after rigid application of the Cartesian axiom, *"de omnibus dubi-*

tandum." It is not simply a set of working hypotheses whose value is pragmatic. It is an ensemble of substantive truths, a structure of basic knowledge, an order of elementary affirmations that reflect realities inherent in the order of existence. It occupies an established position in society and excludes opinions alien or contrary to itself. This consensus is the intuitional *a priori* of all the rationalities and technicalities of constitutional and statutory law. It furnishes the premises of the people's action in history and defines the larger aims which that action seeks in internal affairs and in external relations.

It is to this idea of consensus, I take it, that the Declaration of Independence adverts: "We hold these truths to be self-evident. . . ." I know, of course, that a good bit of sophisticated fun has been poked at this eighteenth-century sentence. But when the sophisticated gentry has had its fun, the essential meaning of the sentence remains intact and its political significance stands unimpaired. The original American affirmation was simply this: "There are truths, and we hold them as the foundations of our political existence as a constitutional commonwealth."

This consensus is the ultimate theme of the public argument whereby American society hopes to achieve and maintain the mark of civility. The whole premise of the argument, if it is to be civilized and civilizing, is that the consensus is real, that among the people everything is not in doubt, but that there is a core of agreement, accord, concurrence, acquiescence. We hold certain truths; therefore we can argue about them. It seems to have been one of the corruptions of intelligence by positivism to assume that argument ends when agreement is reached. In a basic sense the reverse is true. There can be no argument except on the premise, and within a context, of agreement. *Mutatis mutandis,* this is true of scientific, philosophical, and theological argument. It is no less true of political argument.

On its most imperative level the public argument within the City and about the City's affairs begins with the agreement that there is a reality called, in the phrase of Leo XIII, *patrimonium generis humani,* a heritage of an essential truth, a tradition of rational belief, that sustains the structure of the City and furnishes the substance if civil life. It was to this patrimony that the Declaration of Independence referred: "These are the truths we hold." This is the first utterance of a people. By it a people establishes its identity, and under decent respect to the opinions of mankind declares its purposes within the community of nations.

II

The truths we hold were well enough stated. Three are immediate: the limitation of government by law—by a higher law not of government's making, whereby an order of inviolable rights is constituted; the principle of consent; and the right of resistance to unjust rule. These are the heritage of classical and medieval constitutionalism; they center on the idea of law. One truth is remote and metapolitical—that man is not the creature of the City but of God; that the dignity of man is equal in all men; that there are human purposes which transcend the order of politics; that the ultimate function of the political order is to support man in the pursuit of these purposes; that it is within the power of man to alter his own history in pursuit of his own good. You will not find this pregnant truth elsewhere than in the Western and Christian heritage.

Initially, we hold these truths because they are a patrimony. They are a heritage from history, through whose dark and bloody pages there runs like a silver thread the tradition of civility. This is the first reason why the consensus continually calls for public argument. The consensus is an intellectual heritage; it may be lost to mind or deformed in the mind. Its final depository is the public mind. This is indeed a perilous place to deposit what ought to be kept safe; for the public mind is exposed to the corrosive rust of skepticism, to the predatory moths of deceitful *doxai* (in Plato's sense), and to the incessant thieveries of forgetfulness. Therefore the consensus can only be preserved in the public mind by argument. High argument alone will keep it alive, in the vital state of being "held."

Second, we hold these truths because they are true. They have been found in the structure of reality by that dialectic of observation and reflection which is called philosophy. But as the achievement of reason and experience the consensus again presents itself for argument. Its vitality depends on a constant scrutiny of political experience, as this experience widens with the developing—or possibly the decaying—life of man in society. Only at the price of this continued contact with experience will a constitutional tradition continue to be "held," as real knowledge and not simply as a structure of prejudice. However, the tradition, or the consensus, is not a mere record of experience. It is experience illumined by principle, given a construction by a process of philosophical reflection. In the public argument there must consequently be a continued recurrence to first principles. Otherwise the consensus may come to seem simply a projection of ephemeral experience, a passing shadow on the vanishing backdrop of some given historical scene, without the permanence proper to truths that are "held."

On both of these titles, as a heritage and as a public philosophy, the American consensus needs to be constantly argued. If the public argument dies from disinterest, or subsides into the angry mutterings of polemic, or rises to the shrillness of hysteria, or trails off into positivistic triviality, or gets lost in a morass of semantics, you may be sure that the barbarian is at the gates of the City.

The barbarian need not appear in bearskins with a club in hand. He may wear a Brooks Brothers suit and carry a ball-point pen with which to write his advertising copy. In fact, even beneath the academic gown there may lurk a child of the wilderness, untutored in the high tradition of civility, who goes busily and happily about his work, a domesticated and law-abiding man, engaged in the construction of a philosophy to put an end to all philosophy, and thus put an end to the possibility of a vital consensus and to civility itself. This is perennially the work of the barbarian, to undermine rational standards of judgment, to corrupt the inherited intuitive wisdom by which the people have always lived, and to do this not by spreading new beliefs but by creating a climate of doubt and bewilderment in which clarity about the larger aims of life is dimmed and the self-confidence of the people is destroyed, so that finally what you have is the impotent nihilism of the "generation of the third eye," now presently appearing on our university campuses. (One is, I take it, on the brink of impotence and nihilism when one begins to be aware of one's own awareness of what one is doing, saying, thinking. This is the paralysis of all serious thought; it is likewise the destruction of all the spontaneities of love.)

The barbarian may be the eighteenth-century philosopher, who neither anticipated nor desired the brutalities of the Revolution with its Committee on the Public Safety, but who prepared the

ways for the Revolution by creating a vacuum
which he was not able to fill. Today the barbarian
is the man who makes open and explicit the rejection of the traditional role of reason and logic in
human affairs. He is the man who reduces all
spiritual and moral questions to the test of practical results or to an analysis of language or to
decision in terms of individual subjective feeling.

It is a Christian theological intuition, confirmed
by all of historical experience, that man lives both
his personal and his social life always more or less
close to the brink of barbarism, threatened not only
by the disintegrations of physical illness and by
the disorganizations of mental imbalance, but also
by the decadence of moral corruption and the political chaos of formlessness or the moral chaos of
tyranny. Society is rescued from chaos only by a
few men, not by the many. *Paucis humanum vivit
genus.* It is only the few who understand the disciplines of civility and are able to sustain them in
being and thus hold in check the forces of barbarism that are always threatening to force the gates
of the City. To say this is not, of course, to endorse
the concept of the fascist élite—a barbarous concept, if ever there was one. It is only to recall a
lesson of history to which our own era of mass
civilization may well attend. We have not been
behind our forebears in devising both gross and
subtle ways of massacring ancient civilities.

Barbarism is not, I repeat, the forest primeval
with all its relatively simple savageries. Barbarism

has long had its definition, resumed by St. Thomas after Aristotle. It is the lack of reasonable conversation according to reasonable laws. Here the word "conversation" has its twofold Latin sense. It means living together and talking together.

Barbarism threatens when men cease to live together according to reason, embodied in law and custom, and incorporated in a web of institutions that sufficiently reveal rational influences, even though they are not, and cannot be, wholly rational. Society becomes barbarian when men are huddled together under the rule of force and fear; when economic interests assume the primacy over higher values; when material standards of mass and quantity crush out the values of quality and excellence; when technology assumes an autonomous existence and embarks on a course of unlimited self-exploitation without purposeful guidance from the higher disciplines of politics and morals (one thinks of Cape Canaveral); when the state reaches the paradoxical point of being everywhere intrusive and also impotent, possessed of immense power and powerless to achieve rational ends; when the ways of men come under the sway of the instinctual, the impulsive, the compulsive. When things like this happen, barbarism is abroad, whatever the surface impressions of urbanity. Men have ceased to live together according to reasonable laws.

Barbarism likewise threatens when men cease to talk together according to reasonable laws.

There are laws of argument, the observance of which is imperative if discourse is to be civilized. Argument ceases to be civil when it is dominated by passion and prejudice; when its vocabulary becomes solipsist, premised on the theory that my insight is mine alone and cannot be shared; when dialogue gives way to a series of monologues; when the parties to the conversation cease to listen to one another, or hear only what they want to hear, or see the other's argument only through the screen of their own categories; when defiance is flung to the basic ontological principle of all ordered discourse, which asserts that Reality is an analogical structure, within which there are variant modes of reality, to each of which there corresponds a distinctive method of thought that imposes on argument its own special rules. When things like this happen men cannot be locked together in argument. Conversation becomes merely quarrelsome or querulous. Civility dies with the death of the dialogue.

All this has been said in order to give some meaning to the immediate question before us, *sc.*, whether American society, which calls itself free, is genuinely civil. In any circumstances it has always been difficult to achieve civility in the sense explained. A group of men locked together in argument is a rare spectacle. But within the great sprawling City that is the United States the achievement of a civil society encounters a special difficulty—what is called religious pluralism.

III

The political order must borrow both from above itself and from below itself. The political looks upward to metaphysics, ethics, theology; it looks downward to history, legal science, sociology, psychology. The order of politics must reckon with all that is true and factual about man. The problem was complicated enough for Aristotle, for whom man in the end was only citizen, whose final destiny was to be achieved within the City, however much he might long to play the immortal. For us today man is still citizen; but at least for most of us his life is not absorbed in the City, in society and the state. In the citizen who is also a Christian there resides the consciousness formulated immortally in the second-century *Letter to Diognetes:* "Every foreign land is a fatherland and every fatherland is a foreign land." This consciousness makes a difference, in ways upon which we need not dwell here. What makes the more important difference is the fact of religious divisions. Civil discourse would be hard enough if among us there prevailed conditions of religious unity; even in such conditions civic unity would be a complicated and laborious achievement. As it is, efforts at civil discourse plunge us into the twofold experience of the religiously pluralist society.

The first experience is intellectual. As we discourse on public affairs, on the affairs of the commonwealth, and particularly on the problem of consensus, we inevitably have to move upward, as it were, into realms of some theoretical generality—into metaphysics, ethics, theology. This movement does not carry us into disagreement; for disagreement is not an easy thing to reach. Rather, we move into confusion. Among us there is a plurality of universes of discourse. These universes are incommensurable. And when they clash, the issue of agreement or disagreement tends to become irrelevant. The immediate situation is simply one of confusion. One does not know what the other is talking about. One may distrust what the other is driving at. For this too is part of the problem—the disposition amid the confusion to disregard the immediate argument, as made, and to suspect its tendency, to wonder what the man who makes it is really driving at.

This is the pluralist society as it is encountered on the level of intellectual experience. We have no common universe of discourse. In particular, diverse mental equivalents attach to all the words in which the constitutional consensus must finally be discussed—truth, freedom, justice, prudence, order, law, authority, power, knowledge, certainty, unity, peace, virtue, morality, religion, God, and perhaps even man. Our intellectual experience is one of sheer confusion, in which soliloquy succeeds to argument.

The second experience is even more profound.

The themes touched upon in any discussion of Religion and the Free Society have all had a long history. And in the course of discussing them we are again made aware that only in a limited sense have we severally had the same history. We more or less share the short segment of history known as America. But all of us have had longer histories, spiritual and intellectual.

These histories may indeed touch at certain points. But I, for instance, am conscious that I do not share the histories that lie behind many of my fellow citizens. The Jew does not share the Christian history, nor even the Christian idea of history. Catholic and Protestant history may be parallel in a limited sense but they are not coincident or coeval. And the secularist is a latecomer. He may locate his ancestry in the eighteenth or nineteenth centuries, or, if his historic sense is strong, he may go back to the fourteenth century, to the rise of what Lagarde has called *l'esprit laique*. In any case, he cannot go back to Athens, Rome, or Alexandria; for his laicism is historically conditioned. It must situate itself with regard to the Christian tradition. It must include denials and disassociations that the secularism of antiquity did not have to make; and it also includes the affirmation of certain Christian values that antiquity could not have affirmed.

The fact of our discrepant histories creates the second experience of the pluralist society. We are aware that we not only hold different views but have become different kinds of men as we have lived our several histories. Our styles of thought and of interior life are as discrepant as our histories. The more deeply they are experienced and the more fully they are measured, the more do the differences among us appear to be almost unbridgeable. Man is not only a creature of thought but also a vibrant subject of sympathies; and in the realm of philosophy and religion today the communal experiences are so divergent that they create not sympathies but alienations as between groups.

Take, for instance, the question of natural law. For the Catholic it is simply a problem in metaphysical, ethical and juridical argument; he moves into the argument naturally and feels easy amid its complexities. For the Protestant, on the contrary, the very concept is a challenge, if not an affront, to his whole religiosity, to which it is largely alien and very largely unassimilable.

Another example might be the argument that has been made by Catholics in this country for more than a century with regard to the distribution of tax funds for the support of the school system. The structure of the argument is not complex. Its principle is that the canons of distributive justice ought to control the action of government in allocating funds that it coercively collects from all the people in pursuance of its legitimate interest in universal compulsory schooling. The fact is that these canons are presently not being observed. The "solution" to the School Question reached in the nineteenth century reveals injustice, and the legal statutes that establish the injustice are an abuse of power. So, in drastic brevity, runs the argument. For my part, I have never heard a satisfactory answer to it.

This is a fairly serious situation. When a large section of the community asserts that injustice is being done, and makes a reasonable argument to substantiate the assertion, either the argument ought to be convincingly refuted and the claim of injustice thus disposed of, or the validity of the argument ought to be admitted and the injustice remedied. As a matter of fact, however, the argument customarily meets a blank stare, or else it is "answered" by varieties of the fallacy known as *ignoratio elenchi*. At the extreme, from the side of the more careerist type of anti-Catholic, the rejoinder takes this form, roughly speaking (sometimes the rejoinder is roughly spoken): "We might be willing to listen to this argument about the rights of Catholic schools if we believed that Catholic schools had any rights at all. But we do not grant that they have any rights, except to tolerance. Their existence is not for the advantage of the public; they offend against the integrity of the democratic community, whose warrant is fidelity to Protestant principle (or secularist principle, as the case may be)." This "answer" takes various forms, more or less uncomplimentary to the Catholic Church, according to the temper of the speaker.

But this is the gist of it. The statement brings me to my next point.

The fact is that among us civility—or civic unity or civic amity, as you will—is a thing of the surface. It is quite easy to break through it. And when you do, you catch a glimpse of the factual reality of the pluralist society. I agree with Prof. Eric Voegelin's thesis that our pluralist society has received its structure through wars and that the wars are still going on beneath a fragile surface of more or less forced urbanity. What Voegelin calls the "genteel picture" will not stand the test of confrontation with fact.

We are not really a group of men singly engaged in the search for truth, relying solely on the means of persuasion, entering into dignified communication with each other, content politely to correct opinions with which we do not agree. As a matter of fact, the variant ideas and allegiances among us are entrenched as social powers; they occupy ground; they have developed interests; and they possess the means to fight for them. The real issues of truth that arise are complicated by secondary issues of power and prestige, which not seldom become primary. Witness, for instance, Catholic defense of the Connecticut birth-rate control statute.[2] It was passed in 1879, in the Comstock era, under Protestant pressure. Its text reveals a characteristic Comstockian ignorance of the rules

[2] The Connecticut Statute was originally Chapter 78, Public Acts of Connecticut, 1879; it is now Section

of tradition jurisprudence; in general, the "free churches" have never understood law but only power, either in the form of majority rule or in the form of minority protest. Since it makes a public crime out of a private sin, and confuses morality with legality, and is unenforceable without police invasion of the bedroom, the statute is indefensible as a law. But the configuration of social power has become such that Catholics now defend it—with a saving sense of irony, I hope.

There are many other examples. What they illustrate is that all the entrenched segments of American pluralism claim influence on the course of events, on the content of the legal order, and on the quality of American society. To each group, of course, its influence seems salvific; to other groups it may seem merely imperialist. In any

8568 of the General Statutes, Revision of 1949. It reads as follows:

"Use of drugs or instruments to prevent conception. Any person who shall use any drug, medicinal article or instrument for the purpose of preventing conception shall be fined not less than fifty dollars or imprisoned not less than sixty days nor more than one year or be both fined and imprisoned."

Two decisions have been handed down by the Connecticut Supreme Court of Errors (*State* v. *Nelson*, 126 Conn. 412 [1940]; and *Tileston* v. *Ullman*, 129 Conn. 84 [1942]). Both actions were brought, not under the statute itself, but under the general accessory statute (Section 8875, Revision of 1949). Both decisions carried by a vote of three to two.

case, the forces at work are not simply intellectual; they are also passionate. There is not simply an exchange of arguments but of verbal blows. You do not have to probe deeply beneath the surface of civic amity to uncover the structure of passion and war.

There is the ancient resentment of the Jew, who has for centuries been dependent for his existence on the good will, often not forthcoming, of a Christian community. Now in America, where he has acquired social power, his distrust of the Christian community leads him to align himself with the secularizing forces whose dominance, he thinks, will afford him a security he has never known. Again, there is the profound distrust between Catholic and Protestant. Their respective conceptions of Christianity are only analogous; that is, they are partly the same and totally different. The result is *odium theologicum*, a sentiment that not only enhances religious differences in the realm of truth but also creates personal estrangements in the order of charity.

More than that, Catholic and Protestant distrust each other's political intentions. There is the memory of historic clashes in the temporal order; the Irishman does not forget Cromwell any more readily than the Calvinist forgets Louis XIV. Neither Protestant nor Catholic is yet satisfied that the two of them can exist freely and peacefully in the same kind of City. The Catholic regards Protestantism not only as a heresy in the order of religion but also as a corrosive solvent in the order of civilization, whose intentions lead to chaos. The Protestant regards Catholicism not only as idolatry in the order of religion but as an instrument of tyranny in the order of civilization, whose intentions lead to clericalism. Thus an *odium civile* accrues to the *odium theologicum.*

This problem is particularly acute in the United States, where the Protestant was the native and the Catholic the immigrant, in contrast to Europe where the Catholic first held the ground and was only later challenged. If one is to believe certain socio-religious critics (Eduard Heimann, for instance) Protestantism in America has forged an identification of itself, both historical and ideological, with American culture, particularly with an indigenous secularist unclarified mystique of individual freedom as somehow the source of everything, including justice, order, and unity. The result has been Nativism in all its manifold forms, ugly and refined, popular and academic, fanatic and liberal. The neo-Nativist as well as the paleo-Nativist addresses to the Catholic substantially the same charge: "You are among us but you are not of us." (The neo-Nativist differs only in that he uses footnotes, apparently in the belief that reference to documents is a substitute for an understanding of them.) To this charge the Catholic, if he happens to set store, *pro forma,* on meriting the blessed adjective "sophisticated," will politely reply that this is Jacobinism, *nouveau style,* and that Jacobinism, any style, is out of style in this day and age. In contrast, the sturdy Catholic War Veteran is more likely to say rudely, "Them's fightin' words." And with this exchange of civilities, if they are such, the "argument" is usually over.

I should be astonished if the voice of American Jacobinism—or Nativism, if you will—were not heard somewhere along in the essays that follow. I should likewise be astonished if there were no appearance of the seemingly inveterate Protestant tendency to theologize the First Amendment, to read into it certain tenets of Protestant theological dogma, and then to question the civic status of the Catholic within the community on the ground that he does not "believe in" the First Amendment, i.e., he is not a Protestant.

There is, finally, the secularist (I here use the term only in a descriptive sense). He too is at war. If he knows his own history, he must be. Historically his first chosen enemy was the Catholic Church, and it must still be the Enemy of his choice, for two reasons. First, it asserts that there is an authority superior to the authority of individual reason and of the political projection of individual reason, the state. But this assertion is the first object of the secularist's anathema. Second, it asserts that by divine ordinance this world is to be ruled by a dyarchy of authorities, within which the temporal is subordinate to the spiritual, not instrumentally but in dignity. This assertion is doubly anathema. It clashes with the socio-juridical monism that is always basic to the secularist position when it is consistently argued. In secularist theory there can be only one society, one law, one power, and one faith, a civic faith that is the "unifying" bond of the community, whereby it withstands the assaults of assorted pluralisms.

The secularist has always fought his battles under a banner on which is emblazoned his special device, "The Integrity of the Political Order." In the name of this thundering principle he would banish from the political order (and from education as an affair of the City) all the "divisive forces" of religion. At least in America he has traditionally had no quarrel with religion as a "purely private matter," as a sort of essence or idea or ambient aura that may help to warm the hidden heart of solitary man. He may even concede a place to religion-in-general, whatever that is. What alarms him is religion as a Thing, visible, corporate, organized, a community of thought that presumes to sit superior to, and in judgment on, the "community of democratic thought," and that is furnished somehow with an armature of power to make its thought and judgment publicly prevail. Under this threat he marshals his military vocabulary and speaks in terms of aggression, encroachment, maneuvers, strategy, tactics. He rallies to the defense of the City; he sets about the strengthening of the wall that separates the City from its Enemy. He too is at war.

IV

What it comes to then is that the pluralist society, honestly viewed under abdication of all false gentility, is a pattern of interacting conspiracies. There are chiefly four—Protestant, Catholic, Jewish, secularist, though in each camp, to continue the military metaphor, there are forces not fully broken to the authority of the high command.

I would like to relieve the word "conspiracy" of its invidious connotations. It is devoid of these in its original Latin sense, both literal and tropical. Literally it means unison, concord, unanimity in opinion and feeling, a "breathing together." Then it acquires inevitably the connotation of united action for a common end about which there is agreement; those who think alike inevitably join together in some manner of action to make their common thought or purpose prevail. The word was part of the Stoic political vocabulary; it was adopted by Cicero; and it has passed into my own philosophical tradition, the Scholastic tradition, that has been formative of the liberal tradition of the West. Civil society is formed, said Cicero, "*conspiratione hominum atque consensu*," that is by action in concert on the basis of consensus with regard to the purposes of the action. Civil society is by definition a conspiracy, "*conspiratio plurium in unum*." Only by conspiring together do the many become one. *E pluribus unum.*

The trouble is that there are a number of conspiracies within American society. I shall not object to your calling Catholicism a conspiracy, provided you admit that it is only one of several. (Incidentally, I never have seen the validity of Prof. Sidney Hook's distinction: "Heresy, yes; conspiracy, no." The heresy that was not a conspiracy has not yet appeared on land or sea. One would say with greater propriety of word and concept: "Conspiracy, yes; heresy, no." Heresy, not conspiracy, is the bad word for the evil thing. No one would be bothered with the Communist conspiracy if its dynamism were not a civilizational heresy, or more exactly, an apostasy from civilization.)

Perhaps then our problem today is somehow to make the four great conspiracies among us conspire into one conspiracy that will be American society—civil, just, free, peaceful, one.

Can this problem be solved? My own expectations are modest and minimal. It seems to be the lesson of history that men are usually governed with little wisdom. The highest political good, the unity which is called peace, is far more a goal than a realization. And the search for religious unity, the highest spiritual good, always encounters the "messianic necessity," so called: "Do you think that I have come to bring peace on earth? No, but rather dissension (*diamerismon*)" (Luke 12:51). In the same text the dissension was predicted with terrible explicitness of the family. It has been the constant lot of the family of nations and of the nations themselves. Religious pluralism is against the will of God. But it is the human condition; it is written into the script of history. It will not somehow marvelously cease to trouble the City.

Advisedly therefore one will cherish only modest expectations with regard to the solution of the problem of religious pluralism and civic unity. Utopianism is a Christian heresy (the ancient pagan looked backward, not forward, to the Golden Age); but it is a heresy nonetheless. We cannot hope to make American society the perfect conspiracy based on a unanimous consensus. But we could at least do two things. We could limit the warfare, and we could enlarge the dialogue. We could lay down our arms (at least the more barbarous kind of arms!), and we could take up argument.

Even to do this would not be easy. It would be necessary that we cease to project into the future of the Republic the nightmares, real or fancied, of the past. In Victorian England John Henry Newman noted that the Protestant bore "a stain upon the imagination," left there by the vivid images of Reformation polemic against the Church of Rome. Perhaps we all bear some stain or other upon our imaginations. It might be possible to cleanse them by a work of reason. The free society, I said at the outset, is a unique realization; it has inaugurated a new history. Therefore it might be possible within this new history to lay the ghosts of the past—to forget the ghettos and the autos-da-fé;

the Star Chamber and the Committee on the Public Safety; Topcliffe with his "Bloody Question" and Torquemada with his rack; the dragonnades and the Black and Tans; Samuel F. B. Morse, the convents in Charleston and Philadelphia, the Know-Nothings and the Ku Klux Klan and what happened to Al Smith (whatever it was that did happen to him).

All this might be possible. It certainly would be useful. I venture to say that today it is necessary. This period in American history is critical, not organic (to use Prof. Toynbee's distinction). We face a crisis that is new in history. We would do well to face it with a new cleanliness of imagination, in the realization that internecine strife, beyond some inevitable human measure, is a luxury we can no longer afford. Serious issues confront us on all the three levels of public argument. Perhaps the time has come when we should endeavor to dissolve the structure of war that underlies the pluralistic society, and erect the more civilized structure of the dialogue. It would be no less sharply pluralistic, but rather more so, since the real pluralisms would be clarified out of their present confusion. And amid the pluralism a unity would be discernible—the unity of an orderly conversation. The pattern would not be that of ignorant armies clashing by night but of informed men locked together in argument in the full light of a new dialectical day. Thus we might present to a "candid world" the spectacle of a civil society.

2

A NOTE ON PLURALISM

Reinhold Niebuhr

I

Democracy in the Anglo-Saxon world began with the multiplication of the Puritan sects in the Cromwellian period of the 17th century. These sects challenged the monarchic institution by asserting, in effect, that the order created by absolute monarchy resulted in injustice; they also challenged the validity of that curious blend of Catholicism and Protestantism which had become the established church in Tudor England.

The Cromwellian protectorate did not outlive its founder, and the restoration under Charles II seemed to have annulled all the ferment of Puritan Messianism. But a deposit was left which became the basis for the whole structure of English democracy. It must be credited with two primary achievements: 1) the acknowledgment that parliament was supreme, or at least had the right to represent the nation as a force coequal with the crown; and 2) the idea of a pluralistic society in which unity would be achieved by tolerating disparate religious viewpoints. John Locke's essay on toleration at the end of the century was preceded by John Milton's plea for the abolition of licensing, which amounted to a plea for freedom of thought, and by John Saltmarsh's plea for toleration. Saltmarsh argued that all historical viewpoints are fragmentary and do not exhaust the truth. "For," he said, "my truth is as dark to thee as thy truth is dark to me until the Lord enlightens all our seeing."

The spirit of toleration is an absolute necessity for any pluralistic society, for unless men understand the possibility of error lurking in their truth and are prepared to glean some truth in the errors which they combat, there is no possibility of that "limited warfare" which Herbert Butterfield rightly regards as the basis of a democratic society.

There are those who suggest that religious toleration prevailed only as religious skepticism increased; yet the foundation for tolerance was laid in a religious age. It is only fair to note, however, that most of the proponents of the various religious positions did not really believe in either freedom or toleration. Freedom came to the Western world by the providence of God and the inadvertance of history. Tolerance was an absolute necessity for a community which had lost its religio-cultural unity and could find peace only if toleration and freedom were accepted.

The pluralistic communities may have been

forced to accept democratic conditions as necessary for their own survival, but what was forced upon them proved to be beneficial. It was beneficial because the creative nations of the West are all pluralistic, not only in the sense that they allow for various versions of the Christian and Jewish faiths, but in the sense that the secular protest against religion is also given free play. This secular culture provided not only for scientific inquiry into efficient causes, the pragmatic inquiry into proximate ends, but for moral protest against false religious absolutes as well. One of the mysteries of the religious life is that even the most rigorous montheistic faiths, which subject all human ambitions and ends to the ultimate judgment, nevertheless produced the fanaticism which is the fruit of identifying man's ends and purposes with the Divine Will. Hence, cultures in which there is no secular criticism of historic religions become moribund. The culture of Spain provides an example of this, and even more vividly, the culture of those nations in which Islam has been able to erect a sacerdotal state.

Cultural pluralism is, in short, not only necessary for peace in any community, it is a *sine qua non* for creativity as well. Pluralism has become the basis of free communities in all Western nations. This is true because no viewpoint, either as among the various religions or as between the religious and secular philosophies, is able to exhaust the fullness of truth about life. Secularism, for instance, supplies a needed corrective against false religious absolutes; but without the religious approach to life, secularism tends either to create its own absolutes, as Rationalism did in revolutionary France, or to live in a universe in which no sense of the ultimate meaning of existence is raised and life becomes the search for merely immediate and proximate goals. When this happens, men lose their sense of possessing a dignity which transcends all the immediate and proximate ends of life.

The final vulgarity is to equate the ultimate ends of life with the dubious goal of "happiness" and to equate happiness with creature comforts. Our own nation, despite its so-called religious revival, is today threatened by this kind of vulgarity. It is what creates the ironic similarity between the technocratic culture of the communist world and America's own technocratic approach to life, despite the emphasis we place on the dignity of the individual in our culture and the absence of such an emphasis in the communist culture.

Our own nation is distinguished from Western European nations both by the degree of the pluralism found among us and the assurance that pluralism will be preserved which is guaranteed by our Constitution. The degree of the pluralism is due to the multiplicity of the Protestant sects in America and the very strong influence of both Judaism and Catholicism in our national life. The constitutional guarantee is given in the First Amendment which prevents Congress from passing any law "respecting the establishment of religion or prohibiting the free exercise thereof." This prohibition against political preference for any religion is more absolute than anything known in Europe where even the most democratic governments frequently support a state church.

It is furthermore more inclusive if it is remembered that the same England which initiated the principle of religious toleration waited until the 19th century before it removed political disabilities from Catholics. Significantly, John Milton, the great 17th century apostle of toleration, did not include Catholics in his tolerance. The tardiness of England to make toleration universal must be regarded as the consequence of the Catholic cause's being identified first with Spain and then, during the Jacobin controversies, with France. This circumstance leads us to a valuable insight into the limits of pluralism. It shows that a community must be convinced that religious loyalties do not detract from national unity. Even the most liberal state is jealous of its basic unity. Therefore, religious toleration is in part the by-product of other forces, forces of unity and loyalty, both economic and political; these forces reduce the hazards of religious pluralism. No national community can view the possibility of social chaos or disintegration of the community lightly.

II

While it may be questioned whether the Founding Fathers intended to create, in Jefferson's private phrase, an absolute "wall of separation between Church and State," both the peculiar conditions of American life and the Constitution of the United States have created a more complete separation between the two than is found in any other nation. The secular public school in which there may be some minimal religious observances, such as the saying of the Lord's Prayer, but in which there can be no positive religious instruction, is a distinctly American phenomenon. Most European nations have religious instructions in their schools. If there is a multiplicity of Protestant churches they usually agree at least on a syllabus for common religious instruction. The secularization of education is the price we pay for the rigor with which we separate Church and State. I will hazard the opinion that however steep the price, such a separation represents a gain for our public life since organized religion is bound to be divisive and it is a divisiveness we simply cannot afford. Still it must be admitted that the secularization of education represents a loss for individuals because there is a religious dimension in life, a search of the soul for the point of absolute commitment and submission, without which life tends to become stale and meaningless.

It has been frequently observed, however, that this loss is not very apparent in America; we are more religious, judged in terms of loyalty to local religious congregations, than any other Western nation. But we cannot deny that religion in America tends to be merged with the cults of success and the search for power and happiness. We have therefore a very secular religiosity, frequently bereft of the dignity and the majesty of the historic religions.

Strong reaction to this situation has come particularly from Catholics. The Catholic Church is the only religious community with the strength and cohesion to organize an alternative to the secular public school. The Catholic parochial school is as distinctive an American phenomenon as the public school. It has no European analogues. It has been a means of strengthening the Church and giving it a sense of dignity and worth both in its own self-esteem and in the public esteem. The parochial school system is, of course, maintained purely by the resources of the Church, and probably would not be economically possible if the faithful service of nuns and religious Brothers did not reduce the cost of instruction below the cost of the public schools.

The price which the Catholics pay for this separate school system, now giving instruction to 12 per cent of the nation's student population is of course "double taxation." Catholic parents are not exempted from general school taxes and must add the price of instruction for their children to the general charge. This "double taxation" is regarded by many Catholics as "unjust." My friend Will Herberg admits the injustice but thinks as a matter of prudence it is inadvisable for Catholics to challenge the arrangement at least for the present. My only difference with this viewpoint is to relate justice with prudence more intimately and say that prudence requires that many imponderable factors be weighed in deciding questions of justice.

Among the imponderables we must consider chiefly two: 1) the long tradition of the free public school, supported by tax money. Such traditions cannot be lightly changed without disturbing the public peace. 2) the religious pluralism of America which makes any concession on this point inadvisable. Any tax exemption for Catholic parents or tax support for Catholic schools would open the door to a multiplicity of parochial schools. These would tend to disturb the unity of the nation. The nation can afford some slight deviation from the principle of the common school; it cannot afford the total loss.

There ought to be, of course, some prudential compensation for the "injustice" of double taxation. I should think that any "fringe" benefits to Catholic children and parents, such as free luncheons and common rides on school buses, would be advisable forms of relief; they would neither violate a constitutional provision nor endanger the general pattern of education in which a pluralistic nation does the best it can to "preserve the harmony of the whole without annulling the vitality of the parts."

There is not much point in advising Catholics to refrain from making the ultimate claim of tax support for parochial schools, for from their standpoint this would mean a correction of an injustice they suffer under. There is however a point in asserting that the claim for tax support is likely to be granted only at the cost of terrible political turmoil. There is point, too, in advising non-Catholics that the grant of fringe-benefits would ease the Catholic sense of injustice considerably. It would be an earnest on the part of the non-Catholic majority of its good will and of its recognition that while political complexities make the full grant of "justice" (as interpreted by the Catholic side) impossible, there is always merit in giving proof of good will and in recognizing the reciprocal concessions which must be made by all sides to reach something like a tolerable justice.

PART II: *Church and State*

1

THE CASE FOR SEPARATION

Leo Pfeffer

I

Perhaps the major assumption of American constitutional law is that the framers of the Constitution or of a particular amendment had a specific intent in respect to every question that may reach a tribunal for adjudication. The assumption proceeds further that while this intent may have been imperfectly articulated, or perhaps not specifically expressed at all, yet it lay somewhere in the mind of the framers and with sufficient diligence and ingenuity can be uncovered. Once uncovered, the constitutional problem is solved, for nothing remains to be done but apply the contested law or practice against the framers' intent and it becomes a comparatively simple matter to decide if they coincide or diverge.

Carried to its logical limits, this sanctification for all ages of a specific desire of the original framers smacks of ancestor worship. More important as a practical matter perhaps, it often is little more than pursuit of a phantasm. In most cases it is probable that nobody in 1787, when the Constitution was drafted, or in 1791, when the Bill of Rights was added, or in 1868, when the Fourteenth Amendment was adopted, contemplated, or could have contemplated, the specific issue which the courts in the mid-twentieth century are called upon to decide. Moreover, so many different individuals participated in the framing of a particular constitutional provision or amendment that the discovery of any universal intent with respect to it is close to impossible. The disputed phrase may have meant one thing to the person who drafted it, another thing to the majority of Congress which approved it, and something else again to the majority of the members of the State legislatures or conventions that adopted it as part of the Constitution. When, in 1954, the Supreme Court was called upon to decide whether the Fourteenth Amendment prohibited racial segregation in public schools, it abandoned as impossible its efforts to discover a specific intent in respect to the particular issue before the Court.

Even if a universally held specific intent in respect to a particular provision existed and could be uncovered, a slavish adherence to it in all cases might well destroy the Constitution. It is trite to note that the Constitution is a living document. Were we bound today by the specific intent of the constitutional fathers in respect to every phrase and word in the Constitution, then an instrument written to meet the needs of 1787 could never effectively govern the century of nuclear energy. It is only because the Constitution can be interpreted and reinterpreted to meet the needs of contemporary generations that it has been able to remain viable and vigorous for the century and three-quarters of its existence. The Constitution is dynamic and evolutionary, not fixed and static.

This is certainly true with respect to the Bill of Rights. The last quarter of the 18th century was undoubtedly a period of great libertarianism, but the march of freedom did not end in 1791. Practices then commonplace would today be held violative of civil liberties. The elective franchise is as good an illustration as any. Laws restricting the right to vote to persons owning specified minima of property were common, and all voting was in the open by show of hands. Today the universality of the ballot and the secrecy of the polling place are undoubtedly constitutionally protected liberties of Americans. And this has been achieved without any formal amendment of the Constitution.

All this does not mean that history is without significance in the application of the Constitution to the problems of the day. History is of major significance, but its limitations must be understood. The intent of the fathers of our Constitution is not to be applied as a road map or street directory to find the exact location of a particular solution to a constitutional question. It is and can be no more than a guidepost indicating the road to be taken in search of the solution. We must look to the intent of the fathers for the broad objective, the philosophy, the idea underlying the particular liberty secured by the Bill of Rights rather than the specific details of its application. Our constitutional function is fulfilled when we seek to answer a particular question in harmony with that broad philosophy rather than seek the specific answer itself in the remarks that some member of Congress may have made when the constitutional provision was under consideration.

What Chief Justice Warren recently stated about the guaranty of freedom from cruel and unusual punishments contained in the Eighth Amendment is equally true of all the freedoms guaranteed by the Bill of Rights. "The words of the Amendment," the Chief Justice said, "are not precise and . . . their scope is not static. The Amendment must draw its meaning from the evolving standards of decency that mark the progress of a maturing society."

In respect to racial segregation in the schools, the Court's search to discover a specific intent on the part of those who framed and adopted the Fourteenth Amendment proved fruitless. But unless the thousands who lost their lives in the Civil War had indeed died in vain, the general intent of the generation that adopted the Amendment was to achieve for the Negro a status of full and honest equality as far as humanly possible. With that general intent as a guidepost, I think the Court in 1954 correctly found that in our day full and honest equality could not be achieved in a racially segregated public school system. In this larger sense, I believe, the 1954 decision truly fulfilled the intent of the framers and adopters of the Fourteenth Amendment, and historical interpretation has validity in constitutional law.

It is in this light, I suggest, that the meaning of separation of church and state should be sought. And it is in this light that we must test the validity of the interpretation of the First Amendment set forth by the United States Supreme Court in 1947 in the *Everson* parochial school bus case.

In that case the Court interpreted the provision in the First Amendment that "Congress shall make no law respecting an establishment of religion" to mean that the government may not grant material aid to churches or church schools. This interpretation became and remains the subject of a good deal of criticism from many groups and individuals who claim that the Court misinterpreted the Constitution. According to their view, the original and true purpose of the provision was only to bar the establishment of a particular church as the only state church, or at most to bar preferential governmental aid to a particular church or religious group, but not to bar non-preferential aid to religion generally or to all religious groups equally or equitably.

The practical consequences of this difference in

interpretation are of obvious importance. If the Constitution is interpreted narrowly to prohibit only preferential aid, then it is permissible for Congress and the States to appropriate public funds for the support of religious education so long as all church schools are included in the program without favoritism or discrimination. Also it is permissible for the public schools to teach religion so long as each child in the school is taught his own religion. If the broad interpretation announced by the Supreme Court is adopted, neither government financing of religious education nor religious instruction in the public schools is permissible.

I propose to show that the broad interpretation set forth in the *Everson* case is the one most consistent with the historical development of American democracy, the intention of the fathers of our Constitution, the practice and policy of our Federal and State governments and the decisions of the United States Supreme Court. It is my belief that adherence to this broad interpretation and to the principle of strict separation of church and state best serves the interests of religion, of democratic government and of the people.

II

One of America's foremost jurists, David Dudley Field, in speaking of the opening words of the Bill of Rights—"Congress shall make no law respecting an establishment of religion or prohibiting the free exercise thereof"—said:

> The greatest achievement ever made in the course of human progress is the total and final separation of church and state. If we had nothing else to boast of, we could lay claim with justice that first among the nations we of this country made it an article of organic law that the relations between man and his Maker were a private concern, into which other men have no right to intrude. To measure the stride thus made for the emancipation of the race, we have only to look over the centuries that have gone before us, and recall the dreadful persecutions in the name of religion that have filled the world.[1]

To call the separation of church and state the greatest achievement ever made in the course of human progress may be excusable hyperbole. Nevertheless, I am convinced that the evolution and successful launching of the experiment epitomized in the first sixteen words of the First Amendment is the greatest contribution made by the United States to democracy and human progress.

The experiment was uniquely American. Before its launching the concept of religious liberty and the separation of church and state was unknown for all practical purposes. Probably ever since the institutions of religion and of secular powers were recognized as distinct in human history, the two

[1] "American Progress" in *Jurisprudence*, New York, Martin B. Brown, 1893, p. 6.

have competed for and struggled over human destiny. It had never occurred to any but a few visionaries that it might be wrong for a secular ruler to dictate to his subjects how they should worship God or for priests to dictate to the state how it should conduct its secular affairs. It was the United States alone that conceived and proved the workability of the idea that, as Lord Bryce put it, religious organizations should be "unrecognized by law except as voluntary associations of private citizens."

There are some who contend that the First Amendment's provision against laws respecting an establishment of religion was nothing more than a practical expedient to meet a practical problem. According to this view the prohibition of establishment arose out of the multiplicity of rival and jealous sects that existed among the states in 1791. If the national government were to be permitted to establish a particular denomination as the established church of the United States, each sect feared that some other sect would be favored. Accordingly the sects agreed that no one of them should have the greatly desired treasure of establishment.

This, I submit, is historically incorrect, and entirely unfair both to the religious leaders and to the constitutional fathers. By 1791 most of the religious leaders had no desire for state support; the Baptists, Presbyterians, Quakers, Mennonites, and other denominations had had opportunities to share in the fruits of establishment and had turned them down. While the constitutional fathers undoubtedly wished to keep from these shores the quarreling and the rivalries of the sects and hoped, to quote George Washington, "never again [to] see their religious disputes carried to such a pitch as to endanger the peace of society," their concern went far beyond the merely practical problems of appeasing the multiplicity of American sects. They were concerned with principle, the principle which truly underlies our American democratic system.

This principle has two aspects reflected in the "no establishment" and "free exercise" clauses of the First Amendment. These may be termed briefly as separation and freedom. They are not separate concepts or principles but really two sides of a single coin. The fathers of the First Amendment were convinced that the free exercise of religion and the separation of church and state were two ways of saying the same thing: that separation guaranteed freedom and freedom required separation.

The unitary freedom-separation principle was based upon a dual democratic tradition that had evolved in this country during the century and a half before 1791: voluntariness in matters of belief, and government without inherent powers but limited to those specifically conferred upon it.

The concept of voluntariness in matters of belief has properly been called the great tradition of the American churches. It is also the great tradition of American political democracy. Throughout the writings of the political, religious and cultural leaders of the generation that brought forth our Constitution are innumerable references to the evil, tyranny and inefficacy of coercion in the realm of conscience. This concept was as universally accepted in 1791 as it is today and its incorporation in the First Amendment as the "free exercise" clause was both natural and inevitable.

Equally universally accepted was the proposition that government has only such powers as are delegated to it. On this was predicated the no-establishment clause; for it was almost universally accepted in 1791 that power to intervene in religious affairs was not conferred upon government by the people. The conceptual foundation of the no-establishment clause was the inherent incapacity of political government to concern itself with religious matters. Government, in the words of James Madison—father not only of the Constitution but of the First Amendment—has no jurisdiction over matters of religion.

It was this concept that brought together the two forces most responsible for our libertarian democratic system of government, and particularly our constitutional guarantee of freedom and separation—Protestant dissent and secular humanism. The former was a deeply religious, evangelical, pietist force which started with Roger Williams and was led by such devout Christians as Jonathan

Edwards and George Whitefield, and the latter a non-church affiliated deist force led by Jefferson and Thomas Paine.

These two groups arrived at the common ideological meeting place from two different directions. To the religious leaders the source of all temporal power was God, and He had not seen fit to delegate power over religion to temporal governments. Roger Williams pointed out that the Ten Commandments were written by God on two tablets; on one side were the commandments which concern man's relation to God, e.g. "Thou shalt have no other gods before me," "Thou shalt not make unto thee any graven image," etc. On the other side were the commandments which concern man's relationship to man, e.g. "Thou shalt not kill," "Thou shalt not steal," etc. By placing a line of demarcation between the two tablets God expressed His wish that transgression of obligations between man and man shall be subject to the jurisdiction of man's tribunals, but the relationship of man to God shall be exclusively within God's jurisdiction. Other religious leaders reached the same result through the Biblical text, "Render unto Caesar the things that are Caesar's and unto God the things that are God's."

Defense of separation of church and state has recently been equated by some with defense of secularism and hostility to religion. It is, therefore, appropriate to emphasize that the principle of the separation of church and state was evolved by de-

voutly Christian leaders and thinkers long before
it was espoused by the non-religious or was ele-
vated to a constitutional principle in the First
Amendment. It is also appropriate to cite but a
few expressions of the separation principle by the
deeply religious persons who were the leaders and
founders of their churches in America. Roger Williams, a founder of the Baptist Church in America,
was, of course, the first and best known religious
leader to urge the absolute separation of church
and state on the ground that intrusion by secular
authorities in the area of religion constitutes a
usurpation of God's perogative and an encroachment upon His domain.

The Baptist leaders who followed Williams remained faithful to his teachings. Samuel Stayman,
minister of the first Baptist Church of Boston,
preached from the pulpit that the "jurisdiction of
the magistrate neither can nor ought to be extended to the salvation of souls." John Leland,
Baptist leader in Virginia, wrote a tract in the
same year that the First Amendment was adopted,
which was entitled, "Rights of Conscience and
therefore Religious Opinions not recognizable by
law." In this tract, Leland said that "government
has no more to do with religious opinions of men
than with the principles of mathematics."

Basically, the same thought was expressed by
Isaac Backus, spokesman for the Massachusetts
Baptist Churches at the time of the Revolutionary
War and the Constitution. Arguing against the

use of tax-raised funds for religious purposes, he said: "The free exercise of private judgment and the inalienable rights of conscience are too high a rank and dignity to be submitted to the decrees of councils or the imperfect laws of fallible legislators . . . Religion is a concern between God and the soul with which no human authority can intermeddle . . ."

The Baptists, of course, were far from alone among the religious groups in urging this concept. A few years before the adoption of the First Amendment, the Presbyterian Church, arguing against taxation for religious purposes said:

The end of Civil government is security to the temporal liberty and property of Mankind; and to protect them in the free Exercise of Religion— Legislators are invested with powers from their constituents, for these purposes only; and their duty extends no farther—Religion is altogether personal, and the right of exercising unalienable; and it is not, cannot, and ought not to be, resigned to the will of the society at large; and much less to the Legislature—which derives its authority wholly from the consent of the people; and is limited to the Original intention of Civil Associations.[2]

This quotation from a religious group reflects the thinking and influence of the second force responsible for the religion clause of the First

[2] *American State Papers on Freedom in Religion*, Washington, D. C., Religious Liberty Association, 1949, p. 110.

Amendment, the secular-humanist group, which based its ideological agreement with the religious groups on the social contract of Locke and Rousseau. This theory was widely accepted in the latter half of the 18th century and upon it was based the Declaration of Independence and the Constitution. According to the theory of the social contract, governments, in the words of the Declaration of Independence, "are instituted among men deriving their just powers from the consent of the governed." A government, therefore, has only such powers as are granted to it by the governed. A government seeking to exercise powers not so granted is guilty of tyranny and usurpation, and, according to the Declaration of Independence, "it is the right of the people to alter or to abolish it."

The humanists and deists who found their inspiration in the social contract believed, in the words of Madison, that "in matters of religion no man's right is abridged by the institution of civil society, and that religion is wholly exempt from its cognizance." The reason for this, they argued, is that matters of conscience are by their very nature unalienable and, therefore, jurisdiction over them was not and could not have been assigned to political government in the social contract. The views of this group were epitomized in Thomas Paine's statement in *Common Sense:* "As to religion I hold it to be the indispensable duty of government to protect all conscientious professors thereof; and I know of no other business which government hath to do therewith."

It should be noted that this short sentence contains in it the two aspects of the principle spelled out in the religion clause of the First Amendment —freedom and separation. The reference to the "duty of government to protect all conscientious professors" of religion is reflected in the First Amendment's ban on laws prohibiting the free exercise of religion. The aspect of separation expressed in the constitutional prohibition against laws respecting an establishment of religion is reflected in Paine's belief that government has "no other business" with religion.

In 1786, but one short year before the Federal Constitutional Convention met in Philadelphia, these two sources, the religious leaders and the humanists, joined in defeating a bill introduced in the Virginia legislature the purpose of which was to provide tax funds for the teaching of religion. This bill represents the closest approximation in American history to absolutely non-preferential government aid to religion. It is difficult to conceive of any measure which adheres more closely to the requirements of non-discrimination and equality among sects.

In the first place, the preamble to the bill specifically stated that its purpose was *not* to counteract "the liberal principles heretofore adopted and intended to be preserved by abolishing all distinctions of pre-eminence among the different societies or communities of Christians." (At that time there were no non-Christian societies or communities in Virginia.)

In the second place, the bill provided that every taxpayer should have the right to designate which sect or denomination should be the beneficiary of his payment. To the hypothetical argument that the bill made no provision for non-existent "Turks, Jews and infidels," George Washington, who favored the bill, replied that should Jews or Mohammedans or other non-Christians ever come into Virginia, they could declare themselves as such and "obtain proper relief." Finally, the bill went further in seeking to insure equality and non-preference than any measure before or since proposed, in that it made provision for the non-religious. The bill provided that those who did not wish to support any religion could so indicate to the collector of the tax and their taxes would, in such cases, be used for general non-religious educational purposes.

Despite the fact that the bill was non-preferential it was defeated as a result of the combined efforts of the religious and humanist groups. The major factor in the defeat of the measure was Madison's monumental *Memorial and Remonstrance,* one of the great documents in the history of American freedom. In this Memorial, Madison set forth fifteen arguments against government support of religion. These arguments basically fall into two classes: those predicated on the concept of voluntariness in matters of conscience, and those predicated on the concept that religion is outside the jurisdiction of political government —the two aspects of what five years later was to become the religion clause of the First Amendment. For these reasons the Supreme Court has held that Madison's struggle against the Virginia bill is an important part of the legislative history of the First Amendment.

It has been argued by some that the fact that Madison, who was to draft the First Amendment, opposed non-preferential aid to religion by the Virginia legislature is no indication that he opposed non-preferential aid by the Federal legislature, and therefore his opposition to the Virginia bill is not relevant to a consideration of the meaning of the First Amendment. There are two fundamental objections to this contention. In the first place the fifteen grounds for opposition to the Virginia bill set forth by Madison in his Memorial are almost all equally applicable to any measure for government support of religion enacted by any legislature. The principal reasons for Madison's opposition—that religion is not within the cognizance of political society and that support of religion must always be voluntary —are equally applicable whether a state or a Federal government is involved. In the second place, acceptance of the argument would mean that a stream can rise higher than its source. For, as is well-known, Madison believed that the Federal government has only such powers as are delegated to it by the states, and if the states themselves did not possess the power to use tax funds for religious purposes, the Federal government certainly could not do so.

The defeat of the Virginia bill in 1786 was followed by the enactment of Jefferson's great Virginia Statute Establishing Religious Freedom. This law too reflected the dual aspect of what was later to be the religion clause of the First Amendment—voluntariness and separation. The Act forbade the use of tax funds for religious purposes, whether on a preferential or non-preferential basis, and prohibited such use even if a taxpayer's money were to be paid exclusively to the religion of his own choice.

When, therefore, shortly after the Virginia statute was enacted, the constitutional delegates met in Philadelphia to establish an organic law for the United States, no one proposed that the new government should have power to intervene in religious affairs or to use tax funds for religious purposes whether preferentially or non-preferentially. On the contrary, the constitutional delegates deliberately omitted any reference to God from the document which they framed. This omission later became the source of criticism from some sources, particularly those committed to the few remaining established churches. These critics agreed that the new government should have no power to establish a particular sect or to prefer one sect over others. But they argued that an invocation to God or an acknowledgment of His aid would not be preferential and therefore would appropriately belong in the Constitution. For example, a delegate to the Connecticut ratifying convention (Connecticut at that time still had an established church) urged inclusion of "an explicit acknowledgment of the being of God, His perfection and His providence." This criticism was met by the reply, asserted both by the religious leaders and the humanists, that religion must be free and voluntary and that it is not within the cognizance of political society.

Not only did the Constitution emerging from the Philadelphia Convention contain no invocation to God, but its one reference to religion was the negative one, prohibiting any religious tests for Federal office. This too was a deliberate act and a subject of some criticism. In a number of states the fear was expressed that "the Constitution by prohibiting religious tests opened a door for Jews, Turks and infidels." It was urged that even if the Federal government could not prefer a particular sect or denomination, at least inquiry should be made if a nominee for public office "believes in a Supreme Being and in a future state of rewards and punishment." This, it was argued, was non-preferential and did not favor any particular religion.

This criticism, too, was met on the dual ground of freedom from coercion and absence of jurisdiction. In Connecticut Oliver Ellsworth, later to become Chief Justice of the Supreme Court, replied by stating that "the business of civil government is to protect the citizen in his rights, to defend the community from hostile powers, and to promote the general welfare. Civil government has no business to meddle with the private opinion of the people."

Isaac Backus likewise defended the prohibition on the ground that "nothing is more evident both in reason and the Holy Scriptures, than that religion is ever a matter between God and individuals." Even a minister of the still established Congregational Church, who was a delegate to the ratifying convention, agreed with the ban on the ground that "God alone is the God of conscience, and, consequently, attempts to erect human tribunals for the conscience of men, are impious encroachments upon the prerogatives of God." [3] (Note again the concept of encroachment upon God's domain.)

III

Thus it is clear that even before the First Amendment was added to the Constitution, it was universally accepted that the Congress established

[3] Jonathan Elliot, *The Debates in the Several State Conventions on the Adoption of the Federal Constitution,* 2nd ed. Philadelphia, J. B. Lippincot & Co., 1888, vol. 2, pp. 118-119.

by the new Constitution would have no jurisdiction in religious matters. As Madison forcefully put it, the Constitution did not create "a shadow of right in the general government to intermeddle with religion." As is well known, the people were not satisfied with the Constitution because it did not contain a specific and express bill of rights. In order to obtain ratification, the leaders of the Constitution promised to draft and obtain enactment of a bill of rights as amendments to the Constitution. Recognizing the paramount importance of religious liberty and the separation of church and state, the very first words of the bill of rights thereafter adopted in accordance with this promise were the guarantee of religious freedom and the separation of church and state.

The late Charles A. Beard, one of the foremost historians of the Constitution, in his book *The Republic*, explained the relationship of the religion clause in the First Amendment to the Constitution itself. The "Constitution," he said, "is a purely secular document." It "does not confer upon the Federal government any power whatever to deal with religion in any form or manner . . . The First Amendment merely confirms the intentions of the framers."

What this means practically and specifically, Beard said even before the *Everson* and *McCollum* decisions, is this:

Congress can make no law respecting an establishment of religion. This means that Congress cannot adopt any form of religion as the national religion. It cannot set up one church as the national church, establish its creed, lay taxes generally to support it, compel people to attend it, and punish them for nonattendance. *Nor can Congress any more vote money for the support of all churches than it can establish one of them as a national church. That would be a form of establishment. . . .*[4]

The First Amendment, of course, does not expressly use the term "separation of church and state." That phrase was coined by Thomas Jefferson when he explained the reasons for his unwillingness as President to proclaim religious days of fasting or thanksgiving. Convinced that such action on his part would violate the First Amendment, he said:

Believing with you that religion is a matter which lies solely between man and his God, that he owes account to none other for his faith or his worship, that the legislative powers of government reach actions only, and not opinions, I contemplate with sovereign reverence that act of the whole American people which declared that their legislature should "make no law respecting an establishment of religion, or prohibiting the free exercise thereof," thus building a wall of separation between church and state.[5]

[4] *The Republic*, New York, 1943, pp. 165-166. (Emphasis added)
[5] Saul K. Padover, *The Complete Jefferson*, New York, Ovell, Sloane & Pearce, 1943, pp. 518-519.

There has been some effort to discount this letter as no more than a simple letter of courtesy, dashed off without deliberation or serious consideration of its implications. Actually the reverse is true. Jefferson used the occasion to state a view long and deeply held. In his own words, he wished to express "a condemnation of the alliance between Church and state, under the authority of the Constitution." He considered the letter so important that he submitted it to his Attorney-General, Levi Lincoln, before he sent it. Seventy years before the *Everson* and *McCollum* decisions, a unanimous Supreme Court, speaking through Chief Justice White, quoted this statement and declared that "it may be accepted almost as an authoritative declaration of the scope and effect of the Amendment." The same statement was made by another Chief Justice, Charles Evans Hughes, in his book *The Supreme Court*, written shortly before he returned to the Court.

It has often been urged that the language of the First Amendment is clear; that the phrase "establishment of religion" means only the according of monopolistic status to a particular church, in the sense that the Anglican Church is the established religion of England and Roman Catholicism is the established religion in Spain.

It is, I suggest, a mistake to equate twentieth-century usage with eighteenth-century intent. The term "establish" had a much broader meaning in the eighteenth century than it has today. It was used in a great variety of ways, only one of which was to describe a monopolistic church-state relationship. One of the meanings most commonly ascribed to it was simply as a synonym for support; a church was established if it received governmental support, whether it received it alone or together with others.

The best evidence of this is the American reaction to the Quebec Act of 1774. The purpose of this Act was to accord some privileges to the Catholic Church, principally the right to sue for the collection of tithes. This obviously did not accord a monopolistic status to the Catholic Church; it did not even put it at parity with Protestantism, which still retained principal government favor. Yet the Act was widely attacked in the Colonies on the ground that its effect was to "establish the Popish religion." Sam Adams, for example, in an address to the Mohawk Indians charged the English with having "made a law to establish the religion of the Pope in Canada which lies so near to you." In 1774 the Continental Congress in listing its grievances against Parliament, included the act "for establishing the Roman Catholic religion in the province of Quebec." Later, in an address to the people of Great Britain, it asserted that "the Legislature of Great Britain is not authorized by the constitution to establish a religion fraught with sanguinary and impious tenets."

Madison similarly used the term "establish" in a broad context. In vetoing a bill to incorporate the

Episcopal Church in the District of Columbia, he said in his message to Congress:

> The bill exceeds the rightful authority to which governments are limited by the essential distinction between civil and religious functions, and violates in particular the article of the Constitution of the United States which declares that "Congress shall make no law respecting a religious establishment . . ." This particular church, therefore, would so far be a religious establishment by law, a legal force and sanction being given to certain articles of its constitution and administration.[6]

It is important to note that here again the concept that religion is outside the jurisdiction of government is stated as the foundation and basis of the First Amendment, and that intervention by Congress in religious affairs exceeds its rightful authority and constitutes an act of usurpation.

A week later Madison vetoed a bill giving certain land to a Baptist church. His veto message said:

> . . . the bill in reserving a certain parcel of land of the United States for the use of said Baptist Church comprises a principle and precedent for the appropriation of funds of the United States for the use and support of religious societies, contrary to the article in the Constitution which declares that

[6] J. O. Richardson, *Messages and Papers of the Presidents*, New York, *Bureau of National Literature*, 1900, vol. 1, p. 489.

"Congress shall make no law respecting a religious establishment" . . .[7]

Thus Madison made it clear that an "appropriation of funds of the United States for the use and support of religious *societies*" would violate the First Amendment, whether or not some or all religious societies were the beneficiaries.

That is how the generation that wrote the religion clause of the First Amendment interpreted it. To that generation, the Constitution and the First Amendment meant that as far as humanly possible, the exercise of religion shall be absolutely free; and as far as humanly possible, religion shall be outside of the cognizance of political government.

IV

The American people and the American governments, Federal and state, have willingly accepted this interpretation and policy. The astute observer of the American scene, Lord Bryce, may again be quoted as to the universality of this interpretation. Said Lord Bryce:

It is accepted as an axiom by all Americans that civil power ought to be not only neutral and impartial as between different forms of faith, but ought to leave these matters entirely on one side,

[7] Ibid., p. 490.

regarding them no more than it regards the artistic or literary pursuits of the citizens. *There seems to be no two opinions on this subject in the United States.*[8]

Our government has been faithful to this tradition. True enough there have been deviations. A century ago, Congress decreed that the phrase "In God We Trust" should be placed on our coins, thus overruling the thoroughly considered decision of the constitutional fathers not to invoke the name of God in the organic law of the nation. A few years ago this action was expanded by an act of Congress providing that the motto "In God We Trust" be placed upon our paper currency as well. Congress also declared that those who pledge allegiance to the flag of the United States and to the republic for which it stands, at the same time, in effect pledge allegiance to God, irrespective of what their personal religious convictions may be.

There is a great danger in limiting the broad mandate of a constitutional guaranty of freedom by specific acts or practices not in harmony with that broad mandate. Such a procedure can effectively nullify all civil liberties. Racial segregation in the public schools was widespread in 1868 and continued for decades thereafter. If the test of conduct be applied, the unanimous decision of the Supreme Court in 1954 was at least as wrong as it

[8] *The American Commonwealth*, 3rd ed., 1894, vol. 2, p. 766.

(Emphasis added)

is argued by the proponents of the narrow interpretation the *Everson* and *McCollum* decisions were. In 1798, barely seven years after the Bill of Rights was adopted, Congress, composed largely of the same persons who drafted the Bill of Rights, enacted the Alien Law which allowed the President to deport any alien whose presence be deemed dangerous to the United States. The same Congress enacted the Sedition Act under which persons were convicted and sentenced to prison for criticism of the Federalist Administration far milder than what can today be read almost daily in any Democratic and many Republican newspapers. If this almost contemporaneous practical interpretation of the First and Fifth Amendments were adopted today there would clearly be little left of the Bill of Rights.

As a matter of fact, even measured by the standard of practical interpretation, the religion clause of the First Amendment fares very well, much better than the free speech and press provisions of the Amendment and the equal protection provision of the Fourteenth Amendment. I have no doubt that most of the instances cited in support of a narrow interpretation of the establishment clause are inconsistent with its spirit and intent. But these deviations are minor, almost to the point of triviality. How much has been built on the slender foundation of the almost meaningless inscription of "In God We Trust" on our currency, or upon the fact that it has become customary to add "So help me God" at the end of an official oath. Many of these practices—chaplaincies in Congress, for example—are vestiges of the extreme intervention in religious affairs by the Continental Congress which evidenced no hesitation in legislating on a great variety of religious matters. Many of these practices have never been, and as a practical matter cannot be, subjected to judicial scrutiny in litigation, and I think there is a great danger in assuming constitutional everything that the courts do not and cannot expressly adjudicate to be unconstitutional.

The only instance of governmental support of religion of substantial significance is tax exemption for church-owned property. But it must be remembered that this practice long antedated the First Amendment and that it became established at a time when many of the social functions now considered part of a welfare state—care of the fatherless, the aged, the ill and infirm, the destitute—were performed almost exclusively by the churches. Since the churches performed these secular functions which would otherwise be performed by the state, it was both natural and just that they be relieved of the burden of paying monies which would be used to perform those very functions.

The other oft-cited practices are relatively petty compromises of the broad principle of separation of church and state and are conspicuous only by contrast with the general acceptance of the principle by our people and governments. Far more significant than the presence of the name of God on our coins and stamps is the total absence of any reference to Him in the basic charter of our republic, the ban on religious tests for office, the omission of "to provide for the religious welfare" as one of the purposes for which "We the People" ordained the Constitution, and the omission of taxation for religious purposes as one of the powers conferred upon Congress.

To get a true picture of the acceptance by American Federal and state governments of the broad principle of separation of church and state and their recognition that this principle excludes non-preferential governmental aid as well as preferential governmental aid to religion, two facts should be considered, one relating to Congress, the other to the states.

Almost a century and three-quarters have passed since Congress first convened under the Constitution. During that period Congress has legislated in innumerable areas. It has enacted laws authorizing use of tax-raised funds for practically every form of American public and private endeavor, except religion. Vast sums have been appropriated for every form of secular education, including among others nautical education, nurses' training, home economics, agricultural arts, etc. Yet, during this entire period Congress has never enacted a single measure for the direct, non-preferential support of churches or church schools. Indeed, as far as I know, such a bill has never been introduced into Congress. When efforts were made from time to time to obtain Federal funds for transportation of children to church schools or to finance similar auxiliary benefits, they were never defended or justified on the ground that non-preferential aid to church schools is constitutionally permissible. On the contrary, they have always been justified on the claim that the measures would not aid church schools—except, perhaps, indirectly—but only the children. Is not this 169-year record convincing evidence of the universally accepted view that the Constitution prohibits even non-preferential direct aid to churches and church schools?

The second significant fact is the law and practices of the states. There are 48 state constitutions and 48 state legislatures, each completely independent of all others. Yet in every one of the 48 states it is unlawful to grant tax-raised funds to churches or church schools on a preferential or non-preferential basis. In a number of states it is permissible to use tax-raised funds to pay for the transportation of children to church schools; in a few it is permissible to use such funds to purchase secular textbooks for use by children attending church schools. But even in these states it is conceded that direct grant of public funds to church schools, preferentially or non-preferentially, would be unconstitutional and that payment of bus fares or use of secular books is permissible only because the children and not the church schools are the beneficiaries of the state's aid. How else can this unanimity among the states be explained other than by the universal acceptance of the principle that the separation of church and state bars all governmental aid to churches and church schools?

V

Further evidence of the universality, until recently, of the interpretation of the First Amendment contended for in this paper is found in the relevant decisions of the United States Supreme Court. These have been few—an indication of the secure status of religious freedom and the separation of church and state in the United States. But the few decisions that have been handed down by the Supreme Court are all, without exception, consistent with the view that non-preferential government aid to religion is unconstitutional and at least implicitly inconsistent with the contrary view.

I have already referred to the 1878 case of *Reynolds* v. *United States* in which a unanimous Supreme Court stated that Jefferson's description of the First Amendment as creating a wall of separation between church and state constituted "an authoritative declaration of the scope and effect of the Amendment."

The next relevant decision was in the case of *Cochran* v. *Louisiana State Board of Education*, decided by the Supreme Court in 1930. There the Court upheld the constitutionality of a Louisiana statute providing for use by children in all schools, whether under public or church auspices, of secular textbooks purchased with tax-raised funds. The statute was completely non-preferential; it encompassed church schools of every denomination without preference and without discrimination.

Arguing in support of the statute, the Louisiana Attorney General did not contend that it was constitutional because it was non-preferential and because all church schools were aided without favor or discrimination. On the contrary, he conceded that if the beneficiaries of the state aid were the church schools, the statute would be unconstitutional. His argument for validity was based exclusively on the claim that the statute did not aid church schools but only the children attending them.

The Supreme Court, in upholding the statute, likewise did not do so on the ground that it provided non-preferential aid to church schools but on the ground that the aid was to the children and not to the schools. The Court carefully emphasized that the books supplied to the children were secular textbooks, not religious textbooks; if the books had been religious, the statute would undoubtedly have been declared unconstitutional. Thus, it is clear that the Court did not accept the proposition that non-preferential aid to religion is constitutional.

The next relevant decision of the Supreme Court is the famous 1947 parochial school bus decision, *Everson* v. *Board of Education.* In that case the attorney general of New Jersey, in arguing for the validity of a statute providing reimbursement to parents for the expenses of transporting their children to public and parochial schools, did not do so on the basis that the aid was non-preferential. His argument was exclusively based on the contention that the children and not the church schools were the beneficiaries of the law.

In its 5-4 decision sustaining the validity of the statute, all nine justices of the Supreme Court agreed that if the state aid had been given to the church schools, the statute would have been unconstitutional. All agreed that non-preferential governmental aid to religion is as violative of the First Amendment as is preferential aid.

In its decision, the Court set forth clearly and specifically the meaning of the First Amendment. The Court said:

The "establishment of religion" clause of the First Amendment means at least this: Neither a state nor the Federal Government can set up a church. Neither can pass laws which aid one religion, *aid all religions,* or prefer one religion over another. Neither can force nor influence a person to go to or to remain away from church against his will or force him to profess a belief or disbelief in any religion. No person can be punished for entertaining or professing religious beliefs or disbeliefs, for church attendance or non-attendance. No tax in any amount, large or small, can be levied to support any religious activities or institutions, whatever they may be called, or whatever form they may adopt to teach or practice religion. Neither a state nor the Federal Government can, openly or secretly, participate in the affairs of any religious organizations or groups and *vice versa*. In the words of Jefferson, the clause against establishment of religion by law was intended to erect "a wall of separation between church and State." (Emphasis added)

None of the nine justices expressed disagreement with this interpretation of the First Amendment. It was the fruit of long and careful historical research into the evolution and meaning of the religion clause of the Amendment and since its announcement has become the most authoritative exposition of that meaning.

Within a year after the *Everson* decision was handed down, the Court was called upon to repudiate this interpretation of the First Amendment. In *People ex rel McCollum* v. *Board of Education*, the Court passed upon the constitutionality of a system of released-time religious education in effect in the public schools of Champaign, Illinois. Under this system ministers and religious teachers of the different faiths came into the public schools for one hour a week to teach their respective religious doctrines to the children adhering to that faith.

The argument in support of the constitutionality of the program was based upon the claim that it was completely non-preferential and non-discriminatory. Recognizing that the law was unconsti-

tutional if the Court adhered to its interpretation
of the First Amendment set forth in the *Everson*
case, the attorney for the Champaign public school
system urged the Court to overrule the *Everson*
decision and to interpret the First Amendment as
banning only preferential aid to religion.

This the Court refused to do. On the contrary,
it went out of its way to repeat in full the detailed
meaning of the Amendment set forth in the *Everson* case. It reaffirmed that interpretation and held
the Champaign released time program unconstitutional because it constituted state aid to religion,
and it expressly stated that it made no difference
that the aid was non-preferential and non-discriminatory.

In *Zorach* v. *Clauson,* decided in 1952, the Court
in a 6-3 decision upheld the New York system of
released time religious education under which
children enrolling for religious instruction are
released from public school for an hour each
week to receive such instruction under church
auspices outside the public school building. The
validity of the program was sustained because the
public school system did not finance its operation
nor was it in any way involved therein, but simply
adjusted its own schedules to accommodate the
religious needs of the children.

Although Justice Douglas's opinion contains
some unclear language, indicating a retreat from
the broad language of *Everson-McCollum,* what is
significant is that the Court went out of its way

to reaffirm its adherence to the *McCollum* decision and specifically stated that "government may not finance religious groups nor undertake religious instruction nor blend secular and sectarian instruction . . ." By expressly and unambiguously stating that "government cannot finance religious groups," the Court thus made it clear again that it interprets the First Amendment as barring governmental aid to churches whether preferential or non-preferential.

In *Burstyn* v. *Wilson,* decided in 1952, the Court struck down a New York statute which authorized the denial of a motion picture license to a film deemed "sacrilegious," i.e., one that treated any religion with contempt, mockery, scorn or ridicule. The statute, as interpreted by the New York courts, was completely non-preferential; it treated all religions exactly alike and accorded no preference to any of them. Yet the Supreme Court held that under the First Amendment "the state has no legitimate interest in protecting any *or all* religions from views distasteful to them which is sufficient to justify prior restraint upon the expression of those views." (Emphasis added)

The latest relevant opinion is in *Kedroff* v. *St. Nicholas Cathedral* decided in November, 1952. There the Supreme Court held that under the First Amendment's ban on laws respecting an establishment of religion or prohibiting its free exercise, a state may not intervene in the internal affairs of a religious organization as by deciding which of rival factions represents the true church and the true faith.

To complete the account of Supreme Court cases, two other Supreme Court opinions should be mentioned. These are completely consistent with the interpretation urged in this paper. In *Bradfield* v. *Roberts,* decided in 1899, the Court upheld a grant of Federal funds for the benefit of a hospital controlled by a corporation organized by nuns. The Court held that a corporation is a secular entity, that hospital services available to persons of all faiths and of no faith are not religious and that aid to the hospitals is not aid to religion in violation of the First Amendment. Implicit in this decision is the holding that the Constitution would in fact be violated by a grant of Federal money for *religious* purposes to an institution controlled by a *religious* organization.

The same holding is implicit too in the case of *Quick Bear* v. *Leupp,* decided in 1908. There the Court held that treaty funds held by the Federal government as trustee for Indians who were in fact its real owners could be distributed to private religious schools at the designation of the Indians to pay the cost of their tuition. The decision was based on the holding that the money expended belonged not to the Government but to the Indians. Had it belonged to the Government there is little doubt that the decision would have gone the other way.

These are all the decisions of the Supreme Court

that shed light on the meaning of the establishment of religion clause in the First Amendment. From the first to the last they have been consistent—a consistency, I may suggest, rare if not unprecedented in constitutional law. This consistency on the part of the Court, combined with the unbroken record of Congress in refraining from enacting legislation granting direct governmental aid to churches even on a non-preferential basis, and combined with the universal illegality of such grants-in-aid in the 48 states, establishes, I submit, that from the very inception of the Constitution and the First Amendment it was American principle and policy to keep church and state separated by prohibiting governmental aid to churches, preferentially or non-preferentially.

I am aware that the interpretation I urge here has been criticized—particularly in the law schools —as absolutist and doctrinaire. Undoubtedly suspicion of absolutism even in respect to the fundamental liberties in a free democracy is not unjustifiable, and law school professors, perhaps more than any other group in our society, react vigorously to anything that is doctrinaire. But "reasonableness" too has its dangers. Justice Douglas' opinion in the *Zorach* cases breathes the spirit of reasonableness, yet Justice Douglas concurred in a recent dissenting opinion in which Justice Black called the word "reasonable" "that irrepressible, vague and delusive standard which at times threatens to engulf the entire law, including the Constitution itself, in a sea of judicial direction."

As for myself, I have no objection to reasonableness; it is a vital concept in law. But it has its limitations, particularly where the freedoms guaranteed in the Bill of Rights are concerned. These are majestic commands, expressed in terms of the absolute, as are the majestic commands of the Ten Commandments. It would have been at least incongruous for Moses to have commanded "Thou shalt not kill, subject to the reasonable qualification that in time of war or in case of self defense it is permissible to kill." I think it would have been equally incongruous for the Bill of Rights to have commanded "Congress shall make no law respecting an establishment of religion or prohibiting the free exercise thereof subject to reasonable qualifications and conditions."

Absolutes have their rightful place, especially in a charter of freedoms. They set forth a goal to be striven for, though never fully achieved. If, as Browning noted, our reach did not exceed our grasp there would be no need for heaven. Full freedom cannot be expected this side of eternity. But impairments of freedom should be recognized for what they are, imperfections and the falling short of our goal. When the legislature or any other agency of our government, Federal or state, makes a law or performs an act which impairs full freedom of speech, press, assembly or any other freedom, there rests upon it, I submit, a grave obligation to justify the impairment as unavoidably necessary to prevent a serious danger to the community. Even if it fulfills this obligation, it must ever be recognized that the impairment is in the nature of a necessary evil, to be removed as quickly as the danger that justified it disappears. Certainly it should not be adjudged a good to be emulated and expanded.

So, I believe, should it be with the freedom expressed in the religion clause of the First Amendment. The principle of separation and freedom was conceived to be as absolute as possible within the limitations of human communal society. Only where it was unavoidably necessary to prevent an immediate and serious danger to the security or welfare of the community were infringements on religious freedom to be justifiable, and only to the smallest extent necessary to avoid the danger. Likewise, the separation aspect was conceived to be as absolute as could be achieved, predicated as it was on the concept that religion is outside of the cognizance of political government.

Despite occasional impairments, the American people by and large have been faithful to the obligation imposed upon them by the framers of the First Amendment and have guarded well their precious heritage. Church and state have been kept separate and religious freedom has been preserved.

I am convinced, and I believe history supports

my conviction, that because of the American system of separation of church and state, religion has achieved in the United States a high estate unequalled anywhere in the world. As a consequence of more than a century and a half of separation of church and state, religion has grown in the United States to a point where it is by far the most important moral and spiritual force on the American scene. To appreciate this one need only compare the membership in churches and synagogues today when some 60% of our population is affiliated with religious bodies, with the membership at the time the First Amendment was written when no more than 10% of the population was so affiliated.

Earlier I suggested that a slavish obedience of the specific intent of the constitutional fathers, if it could be ascertained, smacks of ancestor worship. The real test of any broad constitutional principle, including religious freedom and the separation of church and state, is not to be found in the archives at the Library of Congress, but in the dynamic needs of a contemporary free society.

Measured by this test, I submit that the interpretation reaffirmed in *Everson* and *McCollum* is most valid. For implicit in it is the basic assumption of a free society—that the state may not preempt the totality of man's personality and activities. It is an assumption rejected by a totalitarian society, fascist or communist. It may appear paradoxical yet it is really quite natural that in such Communist countries as Poland and Hungary priests should be paid by the state and religion should be taught in the state schools. It appears paradoxical because it is Marxian dogma that religion is an evil which the Communist state is committed to exterminate. It is natural because in a totalitarian society no part of man's life, good or evil, is beyond the sovereignty of the state.

A free society proceeds from a directly opposite assumption. It is the assumption that there are some areas of man's life that are too important and sacred to be assigned to the coercive arm of the state. Foremost of these is the area of the mind and conscience, and above all, of man's relationship to God.

2

THE CASE FOR RELIGIOUS LIBERTY

Wilber G. Katz

I

The term "separation of church and state" is sometimes used with narrow reference, as where it in-
dicates merely a rejection of state "establishment"
of religion. We are concerned, however, with a
broader concept of separation when we discuss the
relation between religion and the free society. We
are concerned with separation of church and
state as a characterization of the general American
tradition of church-state relations. It was apparently with this meaning that the phrase was coined
by Thomas Jefferson in his famous letter to the
Danbury Baptists. Here he spoke of ". . . the act
of the whole American people which declared that
their legislature should 'make no law respecting
an establishment of religion, or prohibiting the
free exercise thereof,' thus building a wall of separation between church and State."

I shall be dealing principally with the restrictions which these clauses of the First Amendment
place upon Congress and which have been held
applicable also to state legislatures by virtue of

the Fourteenth Amendment provision that no person shall be deprived of liberty without due process of law. Even more narrowly, my concern will be mainly with situations in which these Constitutional restrictions are interpreted and enforced by the courts. This view of the subject will leave almost untouched the important areas in which church-state relations do not present justiciable issues.

The word "separation" is not accurately descriptive of the American tradition or of the partial embodiment of this tradition in the Constitution. In one sense, "separation" does suggest the thrust of the First Amendment. The two clauses of the amendment prescribed that religion shall be free from the impact of the power of government, whether that power be exerted to establish religion or to restrain its practice. The amendment insulates religion from both types of political action and in this sense enjoins a separation of church and state. The trouble with the "separation" concept, however, is that on debatable questions the analysis of this concept has little light to throw. It is only when the focus is shifted from "separation" to "mutual independence" that fruitful analysis is possible. The amendment explicitly safeguards the independence of religion from the power of the state, and one may perhaps infer equal concern to safeguard political society from the power of organized religion.

The classic illustration of the inadequacy of the

separation concept is the situation in the armed services. Strict church-state separation would make impossible the provision of religious services on ships, army posts, and in the field. Such a policy would indeed have advantages in relieving the armed services of problems which are often highly embarrassing, problems in the establishment of official religious categories, the apportionment of facilities, etc. But the trouble is that strict separation would deprive members of the armed forces of opportunities for corporate worship and instruction. Strict separation must give way since it would seriously limit the free exercise of religion.

Except for occasional flights of rhetoric, no one contends either that absolute separation of church and state is required by the First Amendment or that such a rule would be desirable. Nor does the concept of separation provide its own principle of limitation. In determining the limits of constitutional separation, it is the concept of religious freedom which provides the criterion. The principle of church-state separation is an instrumental principle. Separation ordinarily promotes religious freedom; it is defensible so long as it does so, and only so long.

The proposition that separation of church and state is an instrumental principle is of increasing importance. The more government activity expands, the greater the difficulty in avoiding unintended restraints upon religious liberty. With expanding public action in areas such as relief and welfare, education, urban development, etc., the more often it appears that to maintain strict separation of church and state would involve hostility to religion and intolerable curtailment of religious freedom.

Direct government restraints or compulsions affecting religion have been relatively infrequent in the last century and have given the courts relatively little difficulty. It is conceded that in some situations legitimate concerns of the state justify invasion of religious liberty. Ritual homicide may, of course, be forbidden and snake handling ceremonies may be suppressed. Courts had a little more difficulty with cases regarding religious plural marriage and compulsory vaccination. Compulsory education has likewise been sustained, notwithstanding the religious convictions of the Plain People that the tendencies of education are corrupting. Sometimes the line has been troublesome to draw. The Supreme Court's vacillation on compulsory flag salutes affords one illustration. Another is the Court's difficulty in dealing with prosecutions for obtaining money by fraudulent religious claims.

The principal area of recent controversy has been the extent of the prohibition of legislation "respecting an establishment of religion." It is agreed that this clause forbids discriminatory support of a selected religious group. But is religion to be free also from government aid which is offered without discrimination? In 1947 the Supreme

Court was unanimous in giving an affirmative answer. Mr. Justice Black's New Jersey school bus opinion contained the now famous statement that "Neither a state nor the Federal Government can . . . pass laws which aid one religion, aid all religions, or prefer one religion over another. Neither can force nor influence a person to go to . . . church against his will . . . No tax in any amount, large or small, can be levied to support any religious activities or institutions . . ." The dissenting justices adopted the same principle and furthermore found it violated by the legislation under attack.

The rule of "no aid to religion" requires the government to be neutral not only as between religious groups but also as between believers and non-believers. This principle of full neutrality has been widely challenged. I shall indicate why I regard it as an authentic part of the American tradition of religious liberty. At present, however, I would emphasize that the consequences of such neutrality are not as threatening to religion as some writers have apparently assumed.

Mr. Justice Black explained that neutrality does not require the state to be in effect an adversary of religious groups. As already noted in the case of the armed forces, the state may do a great deal which appears superficially to aid religions. It may do these things, not because impartial aid to religion or encouragement of religions is an appropriate object of government, but because insistence upon strict separation would limit religious freedom and would thus violate neutrality. This was a ground on which Mr. Justice Black and the majority of the Court defended the extension of free bus service to children attending parochial schools. ". . . we must be careful," he wrote, "in protecting the citizens of New Jersey against state-established churches, to be sure that we do not inadvertently prohibit New Jersey from extending its general State law benefits to all its citizens without regard to their religious belief."

What I have said thus far has been introductory. I have introduced what seem to me the two most important propositions concerning the separation of church and state. First, that separation is a subordinate concept, instrumental to the maintenance of religious liberty. Second, that separation prohibits government action designed to aid religion even if discrimination among religious groups is avoided. We may now consider these propositions and the reasons for them somewhat more in detail. It is convenient to begin with the "no aid" proposition.

II

In defending the rule of neutrality between belief and unbelief, Mr. Pfeffer relies heavily upon the setting and legislative history of the First Amendment. I have already indicated my acceptance of this rule as a component of the modern doctrine of separation, but I do not find unequivocal support for it in these historical materials. For example, Pfeffer cites action taken in the Senate on two proposed formulations which would have limited the prohibition to legislation discriminating in favor of particular religious views. These amendments were voted down and Pfeffer offers this action as evidence of intention to forbid also non-discriminatory aid to religion. The difficulty is that six days later the Senate approved another version which forbade only laws "establishing articles of faith or a mode of worship." In view of this action, I think it is very difficult to say what the Senate finally intended when it approved the version which was ratified by the states.

Professor James M. O'Neill, on the other hand, thinks that the historical evidence compels the interpretation that only establishment in the narrow sense was prohibited. I have to reject this view also. The evidence is highly conflicting and it is possible that an ambiguous expression was intentionally chosen by the conference committee. Such want of candor is not unknown—even in ecclesiastical legislation.

Most of those who have taken part in this controversy underestimate the importance of one factor. It is clear that the Amendment was understood to forbid Congress not only to establish religion but also to interfere with the established churches still existing in several of the states. The general language "no law respecting an establishment of religion" was probably chosen with this end primarily in view. This considerably reduces the force of the textual argument for the broad "no aid" interpretation.

In resolving the ambiguity of the Constitution as to government aid, as elsewhere in delimiting the doctrine of separation, the crucial question relates to religious liberty: Is freedom to doubt a component of religious freedom, and, if so, is it placed on a par with freedom to believe? Father Wilfrid Parsons finds it difficult to conceive that those who profess no religion can appeal to the First Amendment, since, he argues, "this document was solely concerned with religion itself, not its denial." Surely this is too narrow a view. Certainly the American tradition of religious freedom includes freedom to doubt and to deny, and the development of that tradition is toward neutrality between belief and unbelief. Skeptical humanists are entitled to be free not only from coercions and penalties but also from the pressure of government influence in favor of religion. Furthermore, a contrary view would require the state to adopt an official definition of religion, a task which involves obvious risks of discrimination against marginal groups.

I do not base my support of the "no aid" principle upon the ground that religion is a private matter of no concern to the state. I believe, on the contrary, that it is of great concern to a democratic state that its citizens find strong, living roots for belief in human dignity and freedom and for faith in the possibility of responsible self-government. It is by no means clear that such roots are maintainable apart from the influence of the Judeo-Christian heritage. The democratic state is indeed concerned with religion. But it is concerned also that basic convictions should be freely held, and this means state neutrality between competing philosophies and religions.

Since *Zorach* v. *Clauson* it is impossible to say with any confidence just what is the present Supreme Court view on the question of non-discriminatory aid to religion. The *Zorach* case involved the New York public school program of released time religious education. The passage in the opinion which gives particular ground for concern is one which starts out reminiscent of the famous passage which I have quoted from the school bus case. It echoes, "The government must be neutral when it comes to competition between sects," but it omits any reference to neutrality toward unbelievers. This omission, together with the sentence "We are a religious people whose institutions presuppose a Supreme Being" make the present doctrine somewhat obscure. For a believer, our legal institutions do presuppose a Supreme Being, but is it now the law of the land that humanist presuppositions afford no alternative basis for loyalty to those institutions?

The problem of tax exemptions is often thought to furnish a test of the "no aid" principle. Defenders of non-discriminatory aid point to existing tax exemptions as supporting their position. Opponents of government aid, like the *Christian Century,* call for abolition of such exemptions. In my view, the problem is somewhat more complex. If a tax law singled out religious groups for an exemption denied to other non-profit enterprises, this would seem to me to be legislation "respecting an establishment of religion" and therefore invalid. But if the state policy is one of using tax exemptions to encourage eleemosynary institutions generally, it is proper to avoid discrimination against similar religious enterprises by including them within the tax exemption.

Consider, for example, the area of family aid, in which the work is shared by state agencies, religious bodies, and non-religious charities. Since there is no policy favoring government monopoly of this field, tax exemptions and deductions are appropriate means of promoting freedom of individual choice in the support of private agencies. Some churches in particular have strong traditions as to the responsibilities of the group, and with present levels of taxation denial of all deductions or exemptions would seriously handicap religious charities.

III

The problem just discussed has brought us back to the proposition that separation is only an instrumental principle. Sometimes this proposition seems to have been denied, as when Mr. Justice Black said that the wall of separation "must be kept high and impregnable. We could not approve the slightest breach," or when Mr. Justice Frankfurter said, "Separation means separation, not something less." I question whether the justices meant these words in a literal sense. Such statements may have tempted Mr. Justice Douglas to write the passage in the *Zorach* opinion which has puzzled Mr. Pfeffer: "The First Amendment within the scope of its coverage permits no exception; the prohibition is absolute." ". . . so far as interference with the 'free exercise' of religion and an 'establishment' of religion are concerned, the separation must be complete and unequivocal." Justice Douglas may have been slyly chiding his colleagues for their exaggerated statements, for he added: "The First Amendment, however, does not say that in every and all respects there shall be a separation of Church and State."

We have already considered the armed services situation as illustrating the limits of church-state separation. Prisons and government communities like Oak Ridge, Tennessee, are other examples where a degree of government involvement with religion is necessary if religious freedom is to be respected. The same is true where children become wards of the state. Religion can not be ignored when the state arranges for a foster home or for institutional care. In none of these situations has the problem been an easy one—nor has it been easy in relation to Indian tribes. Complete insulation of government from competing religions would have great advantages, but it would also have serious disadvantages. In situations like these the answer never has been a wall of separation high and impregnable.

Schools are another area where the government should attempt to maintain this delicate neutrality, avoiding the use of its power to promote religion—however impartially—and avoiding, at the same time, the promotion of secularism. This is the specific subject for later papers, but let me state briefly the form which the issues take according to my analysis.

First with respect to public schools. At the college level, inclusion of the study of religion in state universities has been accomplished without serious difficulty. Here, as Professor Garnett has said, the function of the teaching of religion "is not to propagate faith but to enlighten it where it exists and to create an understanding of the faith of others in those who have none of their own, or who have a different faith." This involves no violation of the "separation" principle. Indeed, exclusion of religion would be a violation of state neutrality. Only extreme separationists have objected to such instruction or to voluntary programs of religious activities.

Skipping over the high school problem, the difficulties become serious when one turns to the elementary school. Is it possible to devise methods of instruction in religion at this level which will be impartial and will not be vulnerable to the charge that they attempt to propagate faith? If this is not feasible, are there other ways of guarding against the propagation of secularism?

This, I think, is the setting in which one must consider the various types of released time programs of religious instruction. But can a released time program operate without more or less subtle coercions? In the *McCollum* case, the Supreme Court held unconstitutional the Illinois program in which the religious classes were held in the school buildings. In the *Zorach* case, the Court upheld the New York program in which the school buildings were not used. Perhaps this factual difference has some significance on the issue of pressure to participate; but apart from this factor, the cases seem indistinguishable. The *Zorach* opinion reflects sympathy for efforts to prevent the secular public school system from impliedly teaching the unimportance of religion or its irrelevance to weekday concerns. This consideration seems an adequate justification unless the program operates in such a way that pupils feel a pressure to participate. It must be added that the evidence of pressure offered in the *Zorach* case was substantial and disturbing.

I am less impressed with the other principal objection to released-time programs, their alleged divisive tendency. In a pluralist society the normal effort should not be to suppress reference to religious and other differences. If this has to be done in a particular situation, it is because the society is sick. Constitutional rules should not universalize the prescription which may be a temporary and local necessity. Perhaps it would be divisive (as well as educationally rash) to set the great religious Dialogue in the elementary school. But it should not be divisive for students to divide for disciplined study of the parts which their respective traditions have contributed to that Dialogue.

One type of released time which should surely be unobjectionable would be a program the benefits of which would be open to a non-religious ethical society and under which parents could secure the release of their children without any participation in the plan. If such a program would be less successful, that fact would be evidence that the traditional programs succeed only by virtue of built-in pressures of the kind which the First Amendment should forbid.

Turning to problems of parochial schools, we start with *Pierce* v. *Society of Sisters;* in 1925 the Court decided unanimously that parents are unconstitutionally deprived of liberty by a statute which attempts to outlaw private schools, religious or non-religious. The decision was based upon the due process clause of the Fourteenth Amendment without reference to the "free exercise of religion" language of the First Amendment. Only later was it settled that the Fourteenth Amendment "incorporates" the First Amendment liberties. The *Pierce* decision is still occasionally criticized by those who urge that public interest in promoting cultural unity justifies overriding a religious conviction that education in religion and secular subjects should be combined. In the Supreme Court, however, there has been no hint that this view is finding support, particularly since the reversal of position on compulsory flag salutes.

But if government must leave parents free to send their children to religious schools, does the First Amendment permit the government to respect that freedom further by arranging distribution of its various benefits so as to avoid discriminating against parents or students who make this choice? My answer is yes: such efforts to avoid hostile discrimination do not constitute "laws respecting an establishment of religion."

This proposition encounters wide and heated opposition. Sometimes the opposition is qualified, and attempts are made to distinguish between aid to students and aid to schools, between public welfare benefits and educational costs, etc. We must examine these attempted distinctions and also the unqualified position which would forbid all efforts to avoid discrimination against private and parochial schools.

The unqualified position has never been more eloquently expressed than in Mr. Justice Rutledge's dissenting opinion in the school bus case. In this opinion, he said, with the concurrence of three colleagues, "Like St. Paul's freedom, religious liberty with a great price must be bought. And for those who exercise it most fully, by insisting upon religious education for their children mixed with secular, by the terms of our Constitution the price is greater than for others." This arresting metaphor of a price tag for religious liberty makes perfectly clear that for Rutledge, separation of church and state is the primary constitutional requirement. For him, separation dictates the limits of religious liberty, not vice versa.

So far as bus fares were concerned, however, this reasoning was rejected by Mr. Justice Black and the majority, who defended non-discriminatory distribution of "welfare" benefits. Presumably the same reasoning justifies inclusion of parochial schools in school lunch and health service programs. Non-discriminatory provision of secular textbooks, however, would be dubious. But why should one attempt to distinguish between "welfare" and "educational" payments? Is not free education as much a "welfare" provision as free dental care or transportation?

Returning to Mr. Justice Rutledge, one wonders how far he would have pressed his view of a constitutional price tag. Would he have considered the G.I. Bill unconstitutional? Under this law Congress provided educational benefits for veterans and left them free to elect study at church related colleges, or even to pursue training for the ministry. Not even the most ardent separationists opposed this measure and perhaps Rutledge would have agreed that the price of religious liberty does not include sacrifice of these educational benefits. Some have distinguished the G.I. payments as not primarily educational but as rewards for military service. Such a distinction, however, is not available with respect to current programs of science fellowships and other scholarships for college study. Applicants attending colleges conducted under church auspices are not excluded from these programs. Does this cheat the Constitution of its full price for religious liberty? If the answer is no, is this because the government is aiding the student rather than the college?

If this formula justifies such non-discriminatory payments, is the situation entirely different below the college level? Even here there is a federal precedent. Congress appropriates funds for education of the page boys who serve in the houses of Congress and the Supreme Court. For boys choosing to attend a parochial or private school, it is expressly provided that payment shall be made to the school chosen, but at a rate no greater than that provided for public schools of the District. Congress apparently takes the view that discrimination against pages attending parochial schools would unfairly restrain religious freedom. Nor did the draftsman even use the formula of payment to the student.

Here is the central issue as to costs of education presented in microcosm. Close reading of the Supreme Court cases leaves the question open, though the pronouncements against taxation for the "support" of religious schools suggest a prohibition too substantial to be avoided by a mere formula. Many states, furthermore, have constitutions specifically prohibiting grants to sectarian schools. To be sure, such provisions have sometimes been held to permit payments for education in sectarian industrial schools on the ground that the payments were not grants in aid but payments for services. However, in view of the setting of controversy over parochial schools in which many of these constitutional provisions were adopted, one may question whether this reasoning could be properly used to permit a general division of school funds.

IV

One theory has been suggested which might explain the refusal of full religious freedom to groups which believe in parochial schools. This is a theory which interprets the American tradition of religious liberty as much more limited than is usually supposed. Professor Mark De Wolfe Howe has suggested that the general American doctrine has theological presuppositions which are inconsistent with full neutrality among religious groups. He says that we shall not reach the heart of our constitutional problem until we ask "whether the objective of freedom and separation is not so intimately related to an article of religious faith as to make the state a religious partisan when it seeks to attain that objective."

Quoting further from Professor Howe: "Those who support the thesis that each man should be left free by government to follow the faith which his mind and heart prefer, very generally, if not invariably, have in religion, abandoned the belief that an ultimate truth has been revealed for all and, as truth, is binding on all. The political conviction that religious liberty is of profound importance generally bespeaks a Protestant, and very frequently a skeptical, attitude towards the 'truths' of religion. Behind our constitutional provisions there may lie, therefore, an attitude, if not a religious faith itself, which is predominantly Protestant in spirit."

Less tentatively, Professor Howe continues by asserting that the First Amendment "in pronouncing a Protestant belief preserved that belief as a living part of our constitutional heritage." He asks why the well-behaved Episcopalian or Presbyterian of today is so hesitant to pronounce as false the doctrine espoused by his neighbor. He suggests that this hesitancy results neither from tolerance nor from devotion to religious liberty, but from skepticism as "an essential element in the spirit of the latter-day Protestant."

Howe concludes that "It is unlikely that the equality which results from liberty will be attained by any church which is committed, or seems to the bulk of the community to be committed, to the doctrine not only that all men are obligated to seek and follow the truth, but that the truth is to be found in its faith only. This is not because civil government as such is unwilling to perform the political promise contained in constitutions but because performance would entail the violation of religious presuppositions in which the promise is grounded."

I cannot say that this interpretation is unfounded. But in attempting an explanation of the refusal of full freedom in relation to parochial schools, I would emphasize not skeptical hostility to those with dogmatic beliefs but fear of those whose devotion to religious freedom is thought to be questionable. Whether such fears with respect to Roman Catholicism have any basis is, of course, another question. Writings of Father John Courtney Murray, S.J., Jacques Maritain, and others have done much to allay such fears. Father Murray's recent article, "The Freedom of Man in the Freedom of the Church," is a profound exposition of what I shall risk calling a Catholic theory of church-state separation. But the history of this concept of "the freedom of the Church," leaves the anxious Protestant with his doubts.

"Although in the extraordinary condition of these times," wrote Pope Leo XIII, "the Church usually acquiesces in certain modern liberties, not because she prefers them in themselves, but because she judges it expedient to permit them, she would in happier times exercise her own liberty." The same pope declared categorically in an encyclical of 1885, "It is not lawful for the State to hold in equal favor different kinds of religions."

But whatever the warrant for Protestant concerns, do they justify state action which is discriminatory? In the American constitutional tradition, are full freedoms to be denied to those who do not fully believe in them? Courts have faced this question often in cases dealing with radical groups of the left or right. The usual approach has been to penalize acts and not beliefs, and to restrict the expression and teaching of beliefs only in circumstances constituting a clear and present danger of action. How far this approach has been changed in recent years is a matter of debate, but there has certainly been no general reversal. Fears of religious oppression justify vigilance and resistance to acts of oppression. Such fears may account for discriminatory measures; but they do not justify restraint of religious freedom.

To summarize: The basic American principle of church-state relations is not separation but religious liberty. This liberty includes freedom from government aid as well as freedom from restraint. Religious freedom has its limits, but they are not limits set by a principle of separation of church and state.

PART III: *The School Question*

1

RELIGION, DEMOCRACY, AND PUBLIC EDUCATION

Will Herberg

I

There are two philosophies of public education competing for the allegiance of American educators, and the conflict between them is of the utmost significance. The first might be called the Anglo-American philosophy, because it has emerged in the context of Anglo-American social thinking and has remained normative in the Anglo-American world. In this view, the government engages in public education primarily because experience has shown that this is the only way of providing educational opportunities for the great mass of the people. Well over a century ago, it had become quite clear that the older patterns of education were no longer adequate. Conditions were changing. Population, especially urban population, was growing by leaps and bounds; large numbers of people were coming into this country from Europe without any experience or tradition of popular education; and the established agencies of education—schools financed by parents, charity schools, or schools sponsored by religious bodies—that had served under less complex and demanding conditions were breaking down.

It was plain that if the great mass of Americans were to receive any kind of education, and education for the masses had become a matter of great urgency, it would have to be through schools established, financed, and maintained by the public authorities. The government was obliged to do what individual or group effort could no longer hope to accomplish. This was how public (or governmental) education developed in this country, and from the beginning this has been the philosophy behind it.

This philosophy, it is well to note, falls in directly with the principle of *subsidiarity* that has received such emphasis in recent social teaching. The principle of subsidiarity holds that, by and large, the government is justified in taking over a general social function only if it is a function that must be performed in the common interest but cannot be adequately performed by individuals or voluntary non-governmental agencies.

According to this conception, the governmental operation of schools is not something inherent in the very notion of democracy; it is rather a function assumed by the government to meet a great and urgent public need where non-governmental efforts obviously do not suffice. But the government has not preempted the field and was never intended to preempt it. On the contrary, the parents (or whatever agency they choose to represent them) retain their original *prior* right to educate their children and to determine the kind of education they are to receive. Of course, the public school has developed other values and has come to serve other functions in the community, but this remains its primary logic and justification in our kind of pluralistic society.

Public education has very different roots, and is articulated in terms of a very different philosophy, on the Continent. There the advocates of public education have always seen things from the point of view of the state. In their opinion, governmental education has not been, and is not, essentially a device to compensate for the inadequacies of individual or group effort in a field of great public importance; it is a "natural" and intrinsic activity of the state, designed primarily to inculcate a common doctrine and create a uniform mentality among the citizens. The people are the wards of the state, and forming the mind of the younger generation is one of the state's most important responsibilities and prerogatives. The state is in its nature a teaching institution, and public education is its proper and legitimate function.

From this point of view, private individuals and non-state institutions, even the parents of the children who are to be educated, really have no business engaging in education, which is properly a monopoly of the state. Under certain circumstances, non-governmental education might have to be tolerated but it can never be accepted as the exercise of a right, certainly not a prior right. In principle, non-governmental education should be suppressed for being divisive and for attempting to usurp the powers of the state over the public mind. Plato was determined to expel the poets from his commonwealth because he did not want any one to compete with the state in indoctrinating the population with the necessary "royal lies." The old-line Continental liberal feels the same about non-governmental agencies of education. This attitude, though championed by men calling themselves liberals, is clearly totalitarian in temper and direction.

It is a doctrine of ancient lineage. In its modern form, it apparently made its first appearance in seventeenth century France among those who were urging Louis XIV to make his state the guardian of the minds of the people. Lord Acton found the key phrase, *l'état enseignant,* the state as a teaching institution, in the Gallican literature of the time, and by the next century the idea of *l'école unique,* a single school system operated by the state, began to figure in the many projects for reorganizing society of which the philosophers of the Enlightenment were so fond. It was not until the French Revolution, however, that these ideas received institutional embodiment. They became the foundation of the Napoleonic program of national education, and they continued to define the basic attitude of the French "progressive" educators through the nineteenth and into the twentieth century. The laicist movement that ran rampant in the early part of the present century found in this educational philosophy a powerful weapon against the church, and so enthroned it as liberal dogma. A similar development, though belated and much modified by other factors, can be traced in many parts of Central Europe. The notorious continuity between Continental liberalism and the centralizing statist despotism of pre-Revolutionary times is clearly mirrored in its philosophy of education.

Here we have a confrontation of two irreconcilable points of view: one, committed to pluralism and the idea of subsidiarity; the other, to a uniformitarian statism with totalistic pretensions. In actual fact, however, the lines have not remained so clear. The pressure of powerful social forces, especially the church, mitigated the uniformitarianism of Continental education, while in this country a number of factors contributed to blur the pluralistic philosophy on which our system of public education is based.

The most important of these factors was the vast influx of immigrants. The rapid assimilation of these immigrants, coming from cultures very unlike the older American culture, was an urgent necessity if the nation was not to disintegrate into a congeries of nationalities. All the resources of society were mobilized for this purpose, but the burden of responsibility naturally fell upon the public school. The public school was expected to make Americans out of the children of immigrants. Inevitably, therefore, it took on a mind-molding function; it became the government's agency for creating a uniform "American mentality" in the children of the immigrants. The government thus became an ideological agency in a way not contemplated in its underlying philosophy.

This trend was furthered by the outbursts of chauvinism that accompanied the First World War, and by the recurrent waves of anti-foreignism going back to the nineteenth century. It was eagerly exploited by a growing group of liberalistic educators, who were inspired by the Continental idea of the teaching state and were trying to remake American public education in its image. Gradually, the Continental philosophy began to creep into the textbooks, and public education began to be seen as properly the prerogative of the government, because the government alone was entitled to form the mind of the younger generation.

All this eroded, but did not destroy, the older pluralistic philosophy. This pluralistic philosophy received its decisive vindication in 1925, when the Supreme Court declared that an Oregon law requiring all children to attend public schools was unconstitutional. The grounds on which this decision was made are perhaps as important as the decision itself. The Supreme Court affirmed in the most explicit terms "the right of the parents to direct the rearing and education of their children,

free from any general power of the state to standardize children by forcing them to accept instruction from public school teachers only." [1] This was
not merely a decision that children cannot be compelled to attend public schools if they are receiving an equivalent education in other ways. It went
much further: it reasserted, with the authority of
the high court, the old American doctrine that the
"rearing and education" of children is the prerogative of the parents, who have prior right as against
the state; the state has no "general power" to
"standardize children" by forcing them to receive
its particular kind of education.

The decision in 1925 came upon the appeal of
a Catholic school; nineteen years later, in 1944, the
Supreme Court handed down a decision on the
appeal of a parent belonging to Jehovah's Wit-
nesses. Denying the power of the state to prohibit
parents from having their children below a certain age (the child in question was nine) sell religious tracts, the Supreme Court declared, with a
direct reference to the Oregon decision: "It is
cardinal with us that the custody, care, and nurture of the child reside first in the parents, whose
primary function and freedom include preparation
for obligations the state can neither supply nor
hinder." [2] The two decisions belong together as a
charter of the rights of parents and the family over
against the state. It is not without significance that

[1] *Pierce* v. *Society of Sisters*, 45 S. Ct. 571 (1925).
[2] *Prince* v. *Massachusetts*, 64 S. Ct. 438 (1944).

these rights are explicitly grounded in that spiritual dimension of man's being that endows him with freedoms, duties, and responsibilities beyond the control and jurisdiction of the state.

This is the American philosophy of public education. It is not merely an educational theory; it is established constitutional doctrine, reaffirmed by the Supreme Court in two historic decisions.

II

Such fundamental considerations as these make it possible to see the problem presented by the claims of religion and the religious school in our educational system a little more clearly and constructively. Let us consider the problem of the religious school first—I mean not a school teaching religion or theology, but a "private," or independent, school, one engaged in general education under religious auspices. In the first place, it is necessary to recognize that the religious school, just because it is a "private" or non-public school, is not therefore a school of an inferior kind to be grudgingly tolerated perhaps but nevertheless treated as an illegitimate rival of the public school. If what I have said has any cogency at all, the religious school, in our kind of free society, must be regarded as essentially a public institution, though it is not governmentally sponsored and operated. It performs a public function, supplying large numbers of children with an education that is everywhere taken as the equivalent of the education supplied in the public schools. It has full public recognition as an educational agency; its credits, diplomas, and certificates have exactly the same validity as those issued by governmental establishments. It is, in fact, part of the nation's educational system, side by side with the public school.

If this be the case, if the independent school is indeed a publicly recognized educational institution, performing a public educational service, why should it not receive public support? I ask this question not only for schools conducted by religious bodies, which make up the great bulk of the non-governmental sector of education, but also for other so-called "private" schools, which are "private" in their auspices but thoroughly "public" in their function and service. Every non-profit-making educational institution, properly accredited, would fall within the scope of my argument.

It is hard to see how the claim of the non-governmental school to public support on the ground that it performs a recognized public service of great importance to the community can be denied. It cannot be maintained that only institutions publicly managed or controlled are entitled to be called public institutions and to receive public support. This is simply not the case and never has been the case in this country. There have always existed in this country, and exist today, all sorts of institutions—libraries, museums, and the like—that are privately managed in whole or in part, and yet are recognized as public institutions and receive public aid and support. I cannot see why the independent school should not be in the same class. The criterion of an institution's eligibility for public support would reasonably seem to be service to the public rather than direct public management; and by that criterion the independent school is manifestly entitled to public support for the service it renders. In fact, as we know, the independent school does receive a considerable measure of public aid today, and submits to a good deal of necessary public supervision.

The only ground on which the independent school can consistently be denied public recognition and public support is the contention that it is undemocratic and un-American because it withdraws children from the school system operated by the government. This is the line taken by James M. Conant, former president of Harvard, in his influential book, *Education and Liberty*. "The greater the proportion of our youth who fail to attend our public schools and who receive their education elsewhere," Mr. Conant asserts, "the greater the threat to our democratic unity. To use taxpayers' money to assist private schools is to suggest that American society use its own hands to destroy itself." Mr. Conant does not carry his logic far enough: if private schools are really such a menace to American democratic society, they should not merely be denied public funds, they should be outlawed. Perhaps that is what Mr. Conant would like, although somehow he cannot bring himself to say so. His whole argument, however, points in that direction and rests on a conception of democracy far closer to a monolithic state totalism, where no rivals are tolerated in any field which the state chooses to enter, than to the pluralistic system established by the Founding Fathers and reiterated, so far as education is concerned, in the classic Supreme Court decisions I have cited.

I do not think it is necessary to belabor the point any further, but perhaps it might be worth while to stress the conclusion: how we appraise the independent school, and its claim to public recognition and support, depends upon our basic philosophy of democracy and upon our view of the nature of public education in a democratic society.

III

But the religious school, particularly the parochial school, is not merely an independent school; it is also a *religious* school; and for this reason the doctrine of the "separation of church and state" is invoked. What, exactly, is the relevance of this doctrine?

The religious school, whether Catholic or Protestant, emerged as part of the continuing pattern of immigrant adjustment to the new American reality. The public schools to which Catholic parents were required to send their children in the latter half of the nineteenth century were, to all intents and purposes, Protestant schools, claiming to be "non-sectarian" because they were non-denominational within Protestantism. Obviously, no believing Catholic parent could send his child to such a school without violating his religious conscience. Not all Catholic parents were equally concerned, of course; but the Church was deeply concerned, and so were many Catholic lay people. Parochial schools emerged to meet this challenge. They were designed to help preserve the faith of Catholic children, a faith then generally expressed in the ethnic form in which it had been brought to this country by the immigrants from Catholic Europe. At about the same time, conservative Protestant groups, like some of the German Lutherans, for whom generalized non-denominational Protestantism was no Protestantism at all, set up religious schools of their own with very much the same double purpose. The emphasis on the ethnic culture declined as a new American generation appeared, but the religious urgency did not diminish.

In the new century, the prevailing ideology of the public schools, at least in the larger urban centers, became secularistic rather than Protestant. "Non-sectarian" came to mean no longer non-denominational but simply *non-religious*. Religion now began to be systematically extruded from education, and American Catholics began to feel the need for religious schools more insistently than ever, because in their conviction no genuine education was possible unless it was religiously grounded and religiously oriented. Education from which religion had been eliminated, they believed, was not simply education without religion; it was, in fact, education based on the counter-religion of secularism, which may, I think, be accurately defined as the theory and practice of human life conceived as self-sufficient and unrelated to God.

In this conviction about the centrality of religion in education, Catholics are being joined in increasing numbers by Protestants and Jews for whom too an education in principle religionless appears utterly wrong. They also are beginning to look to the religious school as a way out of an intolerable situation. A good deal of this new sentiment for the religious school comes from the deeper stirrings of faith that observers have noted among certain sections of the American people; a good deal too undoubtedly comes from the new role that religion is beginning to play as a vehicle of "heritage" and context of belonging. But whatever the factors involved, and they are more complex than appears at first sight, the religious school is certainly enjoying a new favor among Americans. Protestant religious schools are growing in number and enrollment and are being promoted by denominations hitherto hostile to the idea, while the Jewish "day school" movement is expanding rapidly and is attracting increasing numbers of students from American Jewish families.

The religious school is not, however, the only alternative for people disturbed over what they regard as the religionlessness of the public school. The great majority of concerned Protestants, and even some Catholics and Jews, are renewing attempts to bring religion back to some sort of organic relation with public education. In this, they are not by any means running counter to the American tradition; on the contrary; they are returning to it. For the "fathers" of public education in America never conceived of it as education without religion. "Horace Mann," Culver explains in his study of the distinguished pioneer educator, "was opposed to sectarian doctrinal instruction in the schools, but he repeatedly urged the teaching of the elements of religion common to all the Christian sects. He took a firm stand against the idea of a purely secular education, and on one occasion said he was in favor of religious instruction to the extremest verge to which it can be carried without invading those rights of conscience which are established by the laws of God, and guaranteed by the constitution of the state. At another time, he said that he regarded hostility to religion in the schools as the greatest crime he could commit. Lest his name should go down in history as the one who had attempted to drive religious instruction from the schools, he devoted several pages in his final Report—the twelfth—to a statement in which he denied the charges of his enemies! [3] To many Americans today, as to Horace Mann a century ago, eliminating religion from education means eliminating its essential spiritual principle without which it cannot possibly serve its purpose of developing children into truly human beings. Out of this concern, various plans and programs have been advanced to bring religion back to the public school. Both the religious school and these programs for religion in the public schools raise the bitterly controversial issue of the "separation of church and state" in education.

What does this principle of separation, insofar as it is contained in the First Amendment to the Constitution, actually imply?

It is not for me to attempt an authoritative evaluation of the precise meaning of the First Amendment and of the varying decisions of the Supreme Court relating to it. But one thing is clear: the American people have never intended to make this country into a laic state in the European sense, and the First Amendment does not do so. "We are a religious people whose institutions presuppose a Supreme Being," Justice Douglas declared, speaking for the court in the Zorach case[4] and the American people have always taken some such idea for granted. Neither in the minds of the

---

[3] Raymond B. Culver, *Horace Mann and Religion in the Massachusetts Public Schools*, Yale, 1929, p. 235.
[4] *Zorach* v. *Clauson*, 72 S. Ct. 679 (1952).

Founding Fathers, nor in the thinking of the American people through the nineteenth and into the twentieth century, did the doctrine of the First Amendment ever imply an iron-clad ban forbidding the government to take account of religion or to give support to its various activities. Nor does the practice of the government today recognize such a ban.

The federal government has for many decades been selecting, commissioning, and paying religious functionaries to carry on religious work. I have in mind chaplains in the armed forces. The states are doing the same in the matter of chaplains in prisons and other public institutions. The federal government pays the tuition and expenses not merely of students in church-related colleges but even of theological students in ecclesiastical seminaries—under the G.I. Bill of Rights, where money follows the student wherever he goes. The federal government imposes compulsory chapel attendance on the men at West Point, Annapolis, and the Air Academy.

This list of breaches in the "high and impregnable wall of separation between church and state," which Justice Black assumes to be enacted by the First Amendment, could be continued indefinitely. But the point, I think, is already clear. In the mind of the American people, and in the practice of the American government, the separation of church and state does not mean forbidding the government to cooperate with, or even to assist, religion in certain of its activities. It does mean, of course, that there must be no "establishment of religion"; it does mean that whatever cooperation with and assistance to religion the government engages in must not involve interference in the inner affairs of the churches, and must not be discriminatory: the government may not show partiality as among the various religious groups. And, above all, the government must not go "too far" . . .

How far is "too far"? To this, I think, no abstract answer is possible. Were each of the violations of the rigid separation of church and state to which I have called attention put in the abstract —the government financing religious indoctrination, seminary study, etc.—most Americans would be shocked and outraged; confront the same people with the concrete cases, however, and they are hardly aware that anything relating to the separation of church and state is involved. What is right and proper or what is going "too far" depends largely on how public opinion sees the case in the context of time, place, and circumstance; it cannot be gauged by any general formulas. In this area at least, public opinion has been pretty faithfully articulated, in all its apparent inconsistency, by the series of great Supreme Court decisions beginning with the *Oregon* case a generation ago and continuing through the *Zorach* case in 1952.

The relevance of all this to our double problem of the religious school and religion in the public school is not hard to see. *In principle,* there is no reason why the religious school should be barred from governmental support because of what is said or implied in the First Amendment. And, indeed, it has been receiving a considerable amount of governmental support in various ways, in the form of textbooks, bus transportation, school lunches, and similar "fringe" benefits. But the line has always been drawn at direct assistance, and this, it seems to me, is as far as public opinion is ready to go at the present. For the time being at least and for the foreseeable future, beyond that point is "too far."

Religion in the public schools is a more complex problem. While the great mass of the American people undoubtedly agree with Anson Phelps Stokes that the principle of the separation of church and state "does not and should not imply that it [the public school] is irreligious," and that "every such school should show its sympathy with a spiritual outlook that involves the recognition of God as the Creator of the world and of men, and the Judeo-Christian teaching of our duty to him and our neighbor," [5] it is another and very different thing to implement this conviction. Here as elsewhere it is not so much the "separationist" ban in the First Amendment that stands in the way as the fragmentation of religion in this country, and the hostility and suspicion so rife among

[5] Anson Phelps Stokes, *Church and State in the United States,* Harper, 1950.

the religious groups. The constitutional possibilities are broad enough.

The *McCollum* decision (1948) forbids direct religious instruction of any kind on public school premises, but the *Zorach* decision (1952), four years later, permits public schools to cooperate with religious authorities by adjusting schedules so as to make possible religious instruction off school premises. Moreover, though direct religious instruction in public schools is forbidden, there is nothing to prevent teachers and administrators from consciously creating a genuinely religious atmosphere in the schools that is perhaps just as important as direct instruction. The Denver school system, for example, has developed a program of what is called "intergroup education" in which, through a variety of devices, the public school undertakes to "teach that religion is sacred and that the only attitude to have toward it is one of reverence, remembering at the same time that we are talking *about* religion and not religious indoctrination." [6] This kind of pro-religious education in the public schools is quite in harmony with the doctrine of the separation of church and state as Americans understand it; it is, however, possible only where, as in Denver, the major religious groups manage to get together and agree upon a common program. (It is not without interest that

[6] "Philosophy," *December Festivals,* produced under the direction of the Department of Instruction, Denver Public Schools, 1955.

the resource brochure, *December Festivals,* used in the Denver public schools in connection with Christmas and Hanukkah, was produced with the assistance and support of the Anti-Defamation League of B'nai B'rith.) Where such co-operation among the major religious groups is forthcoming, it should prove possible, and in a number of communities it has proved possible, to reverse the trend and to restore religion to some sort of organic relation with public school education.

There are those who place their confidence in a program of "moral and spiritual values"; many, however, feel that such programs, even when religiously interpreted, are bound to prove inadequate and misleading. President Henry P. Van Dusen of Union Theological Seminary and former Dean Weigle of Yale Divinity School have suggested a "common core" program of teaching religion without sectarian indoctrination; others have looked to various schemes of dismissed or released time to provide a partial remedy. Some years ago this writer advanced the idea of combining pro-religious education in the public school with a greatly improved and extended system of released time—not one hour at the tag end of the week, but perhaps three or five hours a week on a par with other subjects in the curriculum.[7] There are obvious difficulties involved in this proposal, but they are not difficulties raised by the constitu-

[7] "Religious Education and General Education: A Symposium," *Religious Education,* May-June 1953.

tional separation of church and state. They are rather difficulties resulting from the fragmentation, rivalries, and mutual suspicion that characterize American religious life and make it difficult for the genuine religious concern of the American people to receive some form of institutional expression.

The public school system has always been the peculiar care of American Protestantism, yet it is American Protestants who are today most deeply disturbed by the religionlessness of the public school. As long as the "non-sectarianism" of the public schools meant a non-denominational Protestantism, most American Protestants approved of excluding religion from the public school; now that "non-sectarianism" has come to mean non-religion, however, the idea does not seem so persuasive. Protestant concern has been growing in recent years, and Protestant voices have joined the many Catholic and the still few though multiplying Jewish voices being raised. It was President Van Dusen who, not long ago, formulated this Protestant concern in a way that links the two aspects of the problem in their true relation. "Unless religious instruction can be included in the program of the public school," he warned, "[Protestant] church leaders will be driven increasingly to the expedient of the church-sponsored school."

IV

Both the religious school and the various programs for relating religion to the public school raise the same basic problem: how to implement the American people's pro-religious commitment without infringing upon the rights and the freedoms of the individual American, whatever his belief or unbelief. In the abstract, this problem, like all other fundamental problems of life in an open society, is quite unsolvable. The Constitution presumably forbids discrimination among citizens on grounds of religion or no religion, and certainly forbids the forcing of the religious conscience. Shall, then, atheist chaplains be commissioned and maintained in the armed forces by the federal government side by side with Protestant, Catholic, and Jewish chaplains, just because the atheists insist on non-discriminatory and equal treatment? Or perhaps the federal government should abolish the chaplaincy altogether in order to avoid this kind of discrimination? What about Christian Scientists who are compelled to have their children take instruction in the public schools in such matters as the germ theory of disease which violate their religious beliefs? Shall we cut these things out of the school curriculum in order to be truly non-discriminatory?

Minorities must not be oppressed, but majorities have their rights as well as minorities, and if every minority veto on the ground of religious discrimination were to be final and decisive, public life would surely become impossible. Some balance must be struck somewhere, but such a balance obviously cannot be a matter of "principle," nor can it be fixed and frozen in a constitutional provision. It must, of its very nature, be a matter of political prudence, involving ever shifting provisional adjustments of rights and claims. After all, is not democracy (to recall Reinhold Niebuhr's celebrated saying) essentially a matter of finding provisional solutions for unsolvable problems?

I know it is difficult to descend from the realm of abstract political theory to the very concrete realm of political prudence and the provisional adjustment of conflicting claims and interests, but that is precisely what any sound political theory itself requires. The federal government commissions and pays chaplains despite the theoretical discrimination this practice undoubtedly involves, since otherwise what are taken to be the "natural" and traditional claims of the vast majority of the American people would have to be ignored. On the other hand, the tender consciences of the Christian Scientists in the matter of the germ theory of disease can be protected by permitting Christian Science children, upon the demand of their parents, to absent themselves from classes where such obnoxious doctrines are taught, and consequently also to be exempted from examinations in the subject. Do Jews object to discriminatory Christmas celebrations in the schools? Combine them with Hanukkah celebrations, and everybody except a few "separationists"-in-principle is happy. These are not particularly neat solutions—no democratic solution in a free society is ever neat—but they have the inestimable merit of being viable.

Political prudence in a free and open society is not something that can be explicitly formulated; it demands a sense of historical possibility and historical actuality, a feeling for the "grain of history" with which we must act if we are to achieve anything worth while that is lasting. What is this "grain of history" as it affects the problems of religion and education?

It is the pattern of what is felt to be right and proper and what is felt to be going "too far" in church-state relations that has emerged from the changing experience of the American people through the nineteenth and twentieth centuries. And it is not a particularly rational pattern at first sight, or even upon second view. Public opinion holds it is all right to pay chaplains in the armed forces, but not religious teachers in the schools. Public opinion holds it is all right that money should follow the student to whatever (approved) school he chooses to attend if he is a veteran, but not if he is a non-veteran. Supplying religious schools with textbooks is all right, but supplying them with funds for construction of school buildings is going "too far." Compulsory chapel and religious instruction in government-operated army, navy, and air academies is all right, but religious instruction in government-operated public schools is going "too far." And so on.

There is no simple rational principle by which one can distinguish what is felt to be right and proper in the public mind from what is felt to be shocking and improper. It is not reason but history that must be consulted, and one must accommodate oneself to history if one is to live in society. Specifically, it is largely a matter of tradition, prejudice, conflicting group interests, and even the momentary constellation of forces. But so is all democratic politics, and the public opinion on which democratic politics depends.

It will not do to be impatient with such ill-defined vagueness and yearn for rationality and principle. Rationality and principle there must be, or else all discussions of policy degenerate into a blind pragmatism; but nothing can be more misleading, more disastrous, than the notion that rationality and principle can be translated into policy in a simple and unequivocal manner. Rationality and principle are not just reflected, they are refracted, and frequently they are refracted in a broken, fragmentary, and distorted manner, in the actual life of even the best society. It is precisely the "ill-defined vagueness" which we are so often tempted to resent that makes our kind of democracy a free and livable system unlike the suffocating uniformitarianism of the ideology-dominated state. To live in a democracy, we must learn to live with, and even to try to understand, the "caprices" of public opinion, however lacking in rationality they may appear to be. They have their own history, and while their history is not their justification, it gives them their meaning and power.

The point of view I am presenting is the point of view of an historical conservatism. I think it bears directly upon the problems we have been considering. Take the religious school for example. I fully recognize the justice *in principle* of the Catholic claim to public support of parochial schools, even to the point of contributing to the tuition of pupils and the salaries of teachers; yet I think it would be misconceived to press such claims at the present time or in the foreseeable future. It does no good to point to the example of certain European countries, or certain provinces in Canada, where such things are done without any appreciable loss of democracy or freedom of religion. Europe, even Canada, is not the United States, and at this point it is historical tradition— or if you will, historical prejudice—that is decisive. Policy requires principle, but it also requires a prudent and realistic understanding of the possibilities and limits of the historical situation.

Allowing for local variations, it may be said that public opinion today concedes the propriety of extending various forms of auxiliary aid, or "fringe benefits," to independent schools on a par with public schools. It is here primarily that a better balance of justice may be achieved, though not perhaps without some difficulty. Even more difficult, though offering good prospects of success, will be the struggle to obtain equal treatment under whatever federal school aid legislation comes to be enacted—always remembering that federal aid may well come to mean some degree of federal supervision and control. In these efforts, the spokesmen for the religious school will have a great and growing segment of public opinion on their side, especially among the younger men and women who are now emerging in public life.

What can be said about the other problem, the problem of bringing about a new relation between religion and public school education? The need is widely felt, but there seems to be no agreement at all on how it is to be met. What we require today are not elaborate and detailed programs but some measure of understanding and cooperation among the major religious groups, for without such understanding and cooperation no program, however good, has any chance of fair consideration or implementation. Whether such cooperation is possible in the present religious situation may well be doubted; and it is these doubts largely that are driving increasing numbers of Protestants and Jews to what President Van Dusen calls the "expedient of the church-sponsored school."

It will not do to leave the subject without raising one more question. The charge of divisiveness against the religious school and against the introduction of religion into public education is not simply a stratagem of the secularist in his crusade against religion or of the statist against the independent school. It is that, to be sure, but it is something more. It reflects a real concern on the part of large numbers of Americans who are not, and do not want to be, secularists or statists.

Let us recall something of the role that the "nonsectarian" public school has played in giving the American people the national and cultural unity it possesses. Until quite recently, the public school was the primary engine of Americanization, entrusted with the task of converting the children of immigrants into Americans. The immigrant parents, but even more the second generation, quickly realized what the public school was doing and were deeply grateful, for despite all qualms, what the parents wanted more than anything else was that their children become Americans and make their way up the ladder of American life. The public school became almost a sacred object to the American people; it was helping to create Americans, and nothing could be more important. Too often in those days the religious schools were preoccupied not only with providing an education in a religious framework but also with perpetuating the immigrant ethnic culture. They were naturally felt to be divisive and were disapproved of as interfering with the progress of Americanization. Something of the same stigma of divisiveness also attached to any sustained manifestations of religious differences, particularly in education.

Our immigrant past is still too recent for these attitudes to have completely disappeared. Something of them still remains, although they are no longer relevant to American reality. Americanization is no longer a problem in present-day America; aside from the few immigrants who still come into this country, Americans today are born not made. And the religious school has turned out to be almost as efficient an engine of Americanization as the public school itself. Today, the older emphasis on cultural unity, and the older fear of divisiveness, are not merely out of place; they can well become an oppressive force in the compulsive conformity that is increasingly the mark of our other-directed culture. Today, the emphasis should be not on unity, except of course the political unity of the nation, but on diversity. And in the effort to safeguard and cultivate diversity, the religious school has a significant part to play, as have the other manifestations and expressions of our diverse religious traditions.

The religious school is not divisive, because American unity is not monolithic, but essentially pluralistic, and the religious school fits in very well as an American institution into the emerging pattern of American religious pluralism. It is not a threat to the public school, because the public school needs competition for its own good and for the good of American democracy, to which an educational monopoly in the hands of the state is quite abhorrent. The older charges against the religious school and so-called religious "separatism" are rapidly losing whatever point they may once have had, while the service the religious school and the educational cultivation of our religious traditions can render as a source of cultural diversity is becoming increasingly important. Both would seem to have a strong case before the court of public opinion at the present time.

2

RELIGION AND EDUCATION IN A FREE SOCIETY

James Hastings Nichols

I

In the most general terms, American Protestantism for the last four generations has supported a dual system of education. The same generation before the Civil War built up parallel institutions, the American public school and the Sunday School, designed to educate children in secular and religious subjects respectively. Most denominations have maintained some church controlled schools at various levels, but at least at the elementary and secondary level they have with few exceptions elected not to try to compete on a large scale with public education.

From the beginning there have been Protestants who have questioned the wisdom of this policy, but the Protestant community as a whole has supported it and still does. What do Protestants think they are doing educationally in supporting such a system? How do they explain it to themselves? I think we may distinguish two levels of Protestant concern with education, the religious and the ethical. The former is more important and I will treat it consequently at more length after discussing the nature of the ethical concern.

The churchman has an ethical responsibility to nurture the roots of political and social order, whatever the religious affiliations of the members of that political community. In modern industrialized society this means a responsibility to contribute to the education of the whole society. Certain intellectual and moral disciplines are indispensable to the maintenance of modern society, and these must be inculcated as a condition of order, peace, and the maintenance of life itself. I have heard Christians from behind the Iron Curtain who are undergoing severe persecution declare that even so they felt an obligation in conscience to support and obey the government save when conscience was directly challenged, because even the Communist state rules within the providence of God and a bad government is better than anarchy.

We do not need perhaps to press the argument this far. The point is that in America the Christian has a responsibility to contribute to a general education for all citizens of whatever faith and no faith. The Christian also has an ethical responsibility to contribute to the opportunities of each individual to develop skills and responsibilities. The only agency through which the Christian can exercise these civic responsibilities is the public school. He has, therefore, a moral duty to contribute to the maintenance of the public school at an efficient level.

This would still be a civic obligation if the public school was as Godless as it is said to be. In particular the public schools have a unique opportunity, of which they are much aware, to prepare future respect and understanding across class, racial and especially religious lines. The social experience of the American public school has been of enormous value in sweetening the acerbities of this melting pot of religions and cultures. Personal respect and friendship for schoolmates and teachers of other races, nationalities and religions has been a priceless aspect of public school education for millions of Americans. Segregation by religion through childhood restricts this basis for respect and understanding in the society at large.

The primary educational concern of Protestantism, however, is religious. The church has the commission to teach all peoples the good news of God's redeeming acts and purposes. Its chief function is to summon man to a radical reorientation of his life, to a recognition of and obedience to the divine solicitation. Religious faith is not fundamentally belief but belonging. It consists in a personal and corporate relation to God, a relation expressed in and deepened by worship and service.

The nurture of these relations has been conceived by American Protestantism for four generations to be primarily the responsibility of the

Christian congregation and the family as the cell of this congregation. Protestants have never considered the public school competent to perform it. They have conceived it possible, and indeed have found it often to be the fact, that the Christian faith is deepened and clarified in the public school, but the primary tasks of evangelism and nurture are the inalienable responsibilities of the Christian society as such.

But does this pattern not indicate a degree of schizophrenia? How could the churches justify this separation of the religious and secular spheres? I think this dual pattern was accepted because the culture had already been secularized before the public school was invented. You are probably familiar with this process in New England. Seventeenth Century Puritans lived in a religiously integrated culture. As Perry Miller points out, they were at once men of the Renaissance and of the Reformation, interested both in the new science and the Westminster Catechism. The schools taught the Bible and theology as wholeheartedly as the church; and also the classics. But even before the end of the 17th Century, the rising commercial classes grew restive with theology in the schools. The notion of education as preparation primarily for the business world was the predominant one by the mid-18th Century. Franklin and Jefferson argued that religious instruction should be replaced by the teaching of natural morality, what would now perhaps be called "character education." Around this core the useful arts and sciences would be grouped.

In the Revolutionary period, the political and social function of education was also stressed to a new degree. Education should make men useful citizens and give them a taste for liberty. The throngs of new immigrants must be prepared to operate republican institutions and the new west must be saved from barbarism.

As public education got under way in this country, consequently, the compartmentalization of religion, on the one hand, and the political and economic and cultural order generally on the other was well established. The earliest state systems came in Massachusetts, Connecticut and New York from the 1830's. The leading educators of this first generation of the public schools were all agreed that the teaching of morality was the paramount responsibility of the public schools. But this was a morality of natural law, the ethical principles generally acknowledged in the common life, even apart from the church and revelation, although in no way incompatible with the teachings of the latter. The meaning of this typical Protestant parallelism of public school and Sunday School is, I think, that Protestants have accepted the compartmentalization of faith and culture. Many have never been aware of any serious tensions between the two. Those that have been troubled have been unable to make a significant attack on the culture in the interest of the faith.

It is from this viewpoint, I think, that we can best understand the Protestant attitude toward their own church controlled schools. Many Protestant denominations have experimented with parochial schools, but on the whole they have largely given them up on the lower levels. Why? Because they were not different enough from the public schools. Perhaps 90 per cent of the curriculum was and is the same. A church school added courses in Bible and theology and maintained corporate worship, but there was no more penetration and theological interpretation of the secularized economic of political order, or of the new science, than there was in the public school. The church school might look like a return to the religiously integrated school, but in fact it meant just more secular education with a kind of Sunday School instruction superimposed.

While I am in no position, obviously, to give an authoritative judgment, it is my impression that this is just as much the case with the Roman Catholic and Jewish parochial schools as with the Protestant. In curriculum, they are all essentially secular schools preparing students for an essentially secular society. They may also teach religious doctrine and train in worship but these things are not determinative of the structure and categories of the academic disciplines of the curriculum. Again I may be wrong, but I don't think the Jews or the Roman Catholics know how to do this any more than we do. The fight for parochial schools is not a fight for a religiously integrated education, but for a closer juxtaposition of religious teaching, practice and associations with a fundamentally secular education.

Now, it is surely an advantage for Christians to have worship closely associated with study and to be able to treat the religious dimensions of the curriculum fully and without inhibition. It is no doubt better to have the teaching of religious literature and history put on an academic par with arithmetic and geography in the child's work week. I am very glad that there are Christian schools seeking to capitalize on and to develop these possibilities. But on the other hand, it is not clear to me, and I think not clear to most Protestants, that these advantages add up to conspicuous gains over what can be accomplished in the effective cooperation of the Christian home and church with the public school. We have very little substantial comparative studies of this sort, and most of what we have comes from the higher levels, and there I think Protestants are not at all certain that their church colleges are doing a better job of religious education than are the religiously neutral private institutions. For some years the pace in religious instruction on the college level has been set by the religion departments of a few of the best-known non-church-related colleges and universities. The extra-curricular religious organizations at these institutions have proved themselves as effective in Christian nurture as the facilities of many Christian colleges. The evidence, I say, is not adequate for a conclusive judgment, but there are many hints that a more keen and mature religious conviction emerges from the free and open situation where Christianity has to fight for its intellectual life than from the mission compounds where the challenge to Christianity is so far as possible muted.[1]

In the Protestant understanding, in any case, faith is a personal commitment which is not to be had without risk. It is tested and deepened by real choices and genuine temptations. It is like freedom. You don't have it unless you exercise it. How this relation with God is to work itself out in factory and office and politics, in the intellectual and cultural life, is a very difficult and complicated problem in a society effectively organized without reference to God. The public school can provide an excellent initiation to the vocation of the Christian layman in such a society. The best preparation for such a life, I suspect, is not an artificially protected situation, but an arena where there are live options and some risks. This the public school can well be.

[1] The lack of competent comparisons of the educational and religious results of the two systems is curious. Why does not some foundation organize a study of the relative religious effectiveness of the several types of schooling in the three chief religious communities? Conceivably the results might release much of the steam which makes the issue so explosive.

This brings us back to a consideration of the conditions within which public education can fulfill this role in maturing religious faith and what the churches have a right to ask of public education. Here I must dissociate myself from one wing of Protestant opinion—not merely Protestant—which argues that education can be non-theological. This is a view which had some plausibility in the days of Horace Mann and Abraham Lincoln, when the average American spent one year in the public schools learning the three R's. But 20th Century public school education is avowedly dealing with values and loyalties, that is to say, with theology and ethics. And there seems to be general agreement that education is significant in proportion as it deals with theology and ethics. Whatever one may say about the separation of church and state in law, one cannot separate significant education from theology. If the *Everson* opinion is to be given the broad scope sometimes urged, then I do not see how the Court can avoid the consequence that it must instruct the states to back up and get out of education altogether, save in purely technical matters, in order to avoid theology.

But in fact, of course, to say that good public school education is theological is not to say necessarily that it is to be informed by a *specific* theology. That would indeed be an establishment of religion. In the efforts of public school men to formulate what they call "moral and spiritual values," I am not sure that due caution has always been observed on this point. I would welcome the efforts of the schools to inculcate honesty, fairness, decency, courtesy, industry and similar moral traits. But I am most suspicious of any official affirmations of the metaphysical source or sanction of such values in the public school. It seems to me that teachers might well set it forth, appropriately to the ages of the students, that the question of such sources or sanctions is an important and debated one, and perhaps indicate alternative interpretations. But what right does the teacher have to teach a humanist view or a Christian one?

One of the most frequently mentioned proposals, which I am afraid some Protestants support, is that the school should teach the common core of the three chief faiths, the "fatherhood of God and the brotherhood of man." Again I must protest, partly for the sake of the fourth "conspiracy," the secular humanists.

Even among the avowedly religious, however, this "common core," this established theology should be rejected. The assumption is frequently made that one is making a significant affirmation with these slogans, the fatherhood of God, the brotherhood of man. It is all so cheap and easy! A couple of units in a syllabus and the young will recognize God as their father and see His children in all their fellows. If this were the case, over what have Judaism and Christianity agonized for ages? Has it not been precisely because of the extraordinary difficulty of bringing about any reconciliation between man as he is and a holy and righteous God? Is not man in chronic rebellion against the very idea of a God who might make claims upon him? What a price must be paid, and has been paid, to open a way to a filial relation! What walls must be broken down, what entrenched hostility encountered to bring us to real brotherliness. Is it done by reading a pamphlet? No one of the three historic faiths of America would admit to such fatuity. As a common core of religious affirmation, the "fatherhood of God and the brotherhood of man" reduces theology to triviality. The whole question is in what sense and on what basis one could conceivably hold such convictions. There may be fruitful theology and ethical discussion among the three faiths. There is no common core.

What the churches should ask of the public school, it seems to me, is not an integrated education, but precisely an unintegrated education, or, in the language of Robert M. Hutchins, a "continuing dialogue" in which the Christian faith is admitted as a participant. They have a right to ask that information about the great historic religions of the West be taught objectively. There seems to be a growing consensus among school men that this should and can be done if they are not continually heckled by the clergy.

Objective teaching, however, does not mean disinterested teaching. No teacher should teach any subject unless he feels that it is important, that it rightfully claims his and his students' attention and time. In the case of theology a teacher in the public school should seek to convey the sense that capital issues are at stake. He will do his best to present the several options as they understand themselves, just as he would do in the case of social and economic theories. No one, of course, is able to present all the alternatives with equal persuasiveness. For this reason it is a matter of good administration to have teachers of various persuasions working in the same school. And school guidance services should be prepared to refer children to competent leaders of the several religious groups when personal problems arise. Objective teaching means that the teacher works for commitment, but not for a specific commitment. Our culture is not in fact an integrated culture and the academic introduction to it should not aspire to synthesis but to conversation and freedom. I believe that the teachers of the American public school system are, on the whole, qualified to maintain free discussion with genuine respect for religious perspectives.

Active laymen and lay women have provided the backbone of the teaching and administrative staff of public education from the beginning to this day in America. School people have generally been church members in a significantly higher ratio than the population generally. While the statistics are probably beyond investigation, I would not be at all surprised to learn that a majority at all times have been church members. These church members have not generally drawn together as such or studied their vocation together as a Christian service, but they have brought a motivation, a sensitivity, a tone to the whole enterprise which it would scarcely have possessed otherwise. While in terms of explicit theology the churches have been held at arm's length, in terms of the fruits in character and attitude, they have dominated the American public school system.

Up to this point I have attempted a positive statement of how many Protestants understand the education their children are acquiring in the interplay between church and public school. I think perhaps enough has been said at least roughly to place this view in relation to other Protestant views, and to those of secular humanists. Something more needs to be said about the prevailing Protestant attitude to Roman Catholic educational programs. That attitude has been described by Roman Catholic spokesmen and others as grudging and unjust. It is certainly very widely critical.

What is the ground for these reservations? Whereas Protestants think that the possibilities of religious nurture in connection with church controlled and with public schools may balance out closely, and conceivably even to the advantage of the latter, they have been quite clear that extensive church schools can only be built up at the cost of the public schools. They are generally persuaded that the devastating decline of our public school system over a long generation has been due in considerable degree to Roman Catholic resistance to school taxes and unconcern over low standards. Many feel that perhaps the greatest barrier to federal relief has been Roman Catholic political opposition to any strengthening of the common school. They read the steady propaganda from Roman Catholic sources about the "Godlessness" of the public schools and many resent it as calculated slander. They fear the further expansion of Roman Catholic controlled education will mean the further crippling of the public school.

In part, this dislike for the extension of Roman Catholic controlled education is the fear of diversion of limited educational resources. As such this dislike would attach to the development of any large church-controlled system. The Roman Catholic Church is the only one large enough to constitute a national threat to public education in this manner. When Protestants, such as Lutheran or Christian Reformed groups, organize parochial education, they are scrupulous to pay their own bills and not to seek exemptions from tax support for community schools.

But there is still another dimension to this problem. When Protestants are challenged with an argument from "distributive justice," many, at least, I think, hear this with one ear, so to speak.

It seems an artificial formulation of the real problem. The crux of the matter, I think, from the Protestant point of view is not church schools versus public schools. The crux of the matter is free education, the education, in Mr. Hutchins' language, "of the dialogue," and censored education, intellectual segregation from the dialogue.

Roman Catholic parochial education is censored education. It is irresponsible education in the technical sense that it is not subject to the criticism and review of the community. From this point of view, I differ with my friend Will Herberg when he applies the term "public education" to Roman Catholic controlled education. It is as "private" as education can be. It is not merely separated from public review and criticism, but it is separated by a certain sacrosanct halo. It can neither be effectively reviewed in terms of standards of ordinary academic competence, nor can its substantive content be criticized without seeming to attack the Church. These things operate behind censorship and privilege. If the parochial schools were to get one tenth of the critical attention from the community at large which appears in the public press constantly with regard to the public schools, there would be screams of persecution and bigotry and intolerance. But the right of supervision and review by the community at large is indispensable to public education.

This, I think, is why the Protestants are concerned. Roman Catholic controlled education is censored education, and part of a general strategy to establish enclaves of concentrated clerical political power, withdrawn from the democratic determination of policy by discussion. To that degree its graduates are crippled as contributors to the great dialogue of our common life. One cannot force a man to enter into a democratic discussion if he does not believe in democracy or discussion, but does "distributive justice" require that we subsidize his secession from the civic dialogue?

Roman Catholic controlled education seems to me much more serious a threat to the standards of public education than the Amish one-room school houses. The Roman Catholic program is to remove from public scrutiny or community assessment the whole pattern of education of a major section of the population. Roman Catholic education has never admitted any communal right of review or criticism. If Roman Catholic controlled education were free education, open to community scrutiny, open to criticism and correction, if the Roman tradition and practice on religious, civil and political liberty were unequivocally positive, then I think the argument about "distributive justice" would hit home to Protestants. To most American Protestants, I think, or at least a very large group, the expansion of Roman Catholic controlled education means a major threat to the free society. I quote perhaps the leading Protestant churchman of the last generation, who was neither hasty nor a Catholic-baiter, Archbishop Temple, whose judgment was that the Roman Catholic attitude toward liberty was "quite unsatisfactory" judged from the point of view of the political traditions of the English-speaking world.[2]

You may say that this is a Protestant conception of the free society. I admit it. At least in historical origin the American conception of a "free society" is unmistakably Protestant—in fact Puritan. Father Murray has noted that the term is not used on the Continent. I suspect, however, he might have found it elsewhere in the English-speaking world. It was a pattern forged, not by our founding fathers—they were the epigones—but by the Puritans of that 17th Century revolution which Trevelyan has well called the greatest event in English history. Lord Lindsay gave what I think is still

[2] "Their whole attitude to freedom of thought is, to my mind, quite unsatisfactory. They acknowledge that compulsory faith is a contradiction and useless, but they also take the view that if, as in Italy or Spain, only the Roman Church exists on any substantial scale, they are entitled to use the arm of the State to prevent propagation of any other form of belief. The faith of the people in those countries is, therefore, not compulsory; it is just what they have grown up in and their wills consent to it; but neither is it a deliberate choice because alternatives have been shut away from them. In other words, the Roman Catholics treat grown-up people permanently as children and that is a frame of mind which inevitably overflows into politics." *William Temple, Archbishop of Canterbury,* by F. A. Dremonger. Oxford University Press, 1948.

one of the most profound interpretations of the Anglo-Saxon conception of a democratic society in his description of Cromwell's view of the place of discussion in a free society.[3] It rests, he said, on "toleration and recognition of differences, based on the belief that God may speak through any member of the community, combined with insistence that individual views shall submit to the criticism of open discussion." No Roman Catholic society that I know of has ever produced such a conception of freedom,—civic, intellectual, religious. In this sense the American tradition of democracy is still Protestant, and American society promises to become less free in proportion to the growth of Roman Catholic influence on it.

Personally I am not embarrassed at defending this conception, nor do I think that American Protestantism needs to feel embarrassed at defending this conception against a growing Roman Catholic pressure to approximate structures and methods more characteristic of Spain, France or Italy. This untidy ecclesiastical pattern of Puritan denominationalism has maintained more Christian influence on public life than any other Christian tradition in the modern world. It has never, as Roman Catholicism always does, provoked a major militant anti-religious political movement, Marxist or otherwise.

I would like to qualify my observations on the

[3] *The Essentials of Democracy*, London, Oxford University Press, 1930, p. 36.

relation of Roman Catholicism to a free society by another reflection which has more weight with me than with most of my co-religionists. I think that where the Roman community and tradition promises little for the maintenance or strengthening of a free society, it insures some division of power and consequently a measure of liberty in an authoritarian society. In our generation we have seen Germany, Italy and Russia overrun by anti-Christian totalitarian movements. France and Great Britain are both described seriously as Christian mission fields, as "post-Christian" societies. I do not take comfort in the American church statistics. To me they mean that if totalitarian humanism captures America, it will seek to claim the Christian name and the churches will be torn by a great theological *kirchenkampf*. In such an eventuality I think I would be very grateful for the quasi-military discipline of the Roman Catholic Church. To adopt it now, on the other hand, saps the power of the civil community to ward off such a collapse.

In any case, I do not expect to see either communion change its methods or views materially. I admire the efforts of men like Father John Courtney Murray, Jacques Maritain and others, but as an historian I have a high estimate of the inertia of great institutional traditions. I have little hope of significantly arbitrating the present political struggle going on in a thousand communities, of school board politics, of lobbying in legislative halls and committees. It is a struggle for the shaping of American society and culture, founded on deep divergencies on the nature of religious authority and of political virtue. I expect to see the free society lose a good many battles to the authoritarians.

I have been impressed by accounts of the community of righteousness discovered across religious traditions in the times of the recent wars and persecutions. In prison camps, for example, individual Roman Catholics, Protestants, Jews, even secular humanists, have often found themselves unexpectedly comrades against the ultimate challenge to human dignity and to right. Once the pressure was over, however, and the question was that of shaping society rather than electing what to die for, this community fell apart again. But to me that momentary community was a parable of something ultimate. None of us can escape our traditions, few of us can change them very much. Men of sincerity and good will and religious faith regularly find themselves conscientiously opposed to each other. We see in part. But there is One unto Whom all hearts are open, Who can assay all the mortal ambiguities, and Who will in His good time assemble in one community those to whom He has lent the power of righteousness and brotherliness.

PART IV: *The Secular Challenge*

1

THE RELIGIOUS-SECULAR DIALOGUE

Walter J. Ong

I

Viewed historically, pluralism in human society is something which calls for a positive interpretation, not only by those who profess themselves to be religiously uncommitted but especially by the committed who participate in the Christian or the Hebraic point of view, or any point of view which regards God as Master of history. Taken as a whole, this pluralism arises from earlier conditions which are by no means desirable.

I am aware that one can—and some do—consider pluralism as somehow a defection from an ideal supposedly realized in the past, when "everybody" was a member of a united religious as well as secular community, or perhaps when a supposedly other-worldly outlook was universal. From such a state, we are to suppose, there has arisen a pluralistic age of secular depravity almost as universal—save for the remnant who persevere in their stern, self-imposed task of viewing the present with steady and indefectible alarm.

But to consider any model from the past as the

realization of the Christian ideal of unity is to belie this ideal itself. The romantic concept of medieval Europe, which is the model most often resorted to here, will not do at all. According to this concept, European society is taken as a self-sufficient and entirely integral unit threatened only by the incursions of the Mohammedans and Mongols and a few others, who supposedly always took the initiative in aggressiveness and thus made evident their own perversity, thereby also rendering forceless any questions which might arise concerning the real problems of conscience faced by a Christian *vis-à-vis* Islam. In this view Christians are envisioned as living in something called "Christendom," which is taken to be a self-sufficient unity not faced with any real problems outside its own perimeters and in adequate control of the problems within.

The fallacy in this view is that anyone outside the perimeters of Christianity is by that very fact a problem for Christians, since the Christian is a man with the Gospel, the Good News, which is destined for all men and which he is obliged to make known to those who have not heard of it. Thus, ideally a medieval Christianity possessed by ancient memories of the Nestorians in India and China, or later stirred by the voyages of Marco Polo or by the reports of the thirteenth- and fourteenth-century Franciscan and Dominican emissaries to the Mongols, as recently edited by Christopher Dawson, or even by the compilations circulated under the name of Sir John Mandeville, could by no means consider itself a self-contained unit. It was necessarily an incompleteness. However replete with Christianity Christendom might be up to its very boundaries, Christian society was in no real way a complete society until the Good News had been brought to all men.

Of course, it could be urged that effective preaching of the Gospel to lands as little known to Christians as China and India was impossible in the thirteenth and fourteenth centuries. But such a view is open to question. Carrying the Good News to such lands was physically and psychologically difficult, yes, but hardly impossible. Several embassies of Christians had reached the Grand Khan himself. And if such embassies could reach their destination, why might not sizable groups of missionaries have attempted to bring the Good News to the Far East? Kublai Khan's request, reported by Marco Polo, to have a hundred learned Christians sent him to prove the truth of the Christian faith aroused little response in the West.

There was, one might urge, too much to do at home. But there always is. At the very time he was preaching the Gospel elsewhere, St. Paul was writing his letters to the Corinthians and Philippians and Colossians in an effort to straighten out the chaos he had had to leave behind. The fact is that medieval man's vision of the Catholicity of the Church here failed somehow to stir the medieval imagination religiously, even when the presence of Tartar slaves in Europe suggests that the imagination had been stirred to some extent commercially. It may not have been the fault of medieval man, but his vision of Catholicity did leave something to be desired.

The fact is that medieval society was supported not only by the minimal development of communications but also by a more or less conscious effort to shrink what communications there were. This enabled the medieval West European Christian to keep his imagination relatively clear of involvement with persons who were not Christians, as though they did not really concern him. Even granted that this state of mind is quite understandable because of the insecurity of life five or six hundred years ago, it was not in itself a desirable state of mind for a Christian. The state of mind belongs to the medieval age rather than to the Christian ethos. The ghetto was the typical medieval institution maintained by cooperation of medieval Christians with medieval Jews.

Despite the avowedly Catholic mission of the Church, pre-modern Christianity often fell too easily into the habit of thinking of Christendom and of religion generally in terms of geographical divisions and frontiers. Insofar as it did so, it really blinked the problem of coexistence, and indeed of pluralism. For a Christian especially, all mankind is one. If the medieval Christian had faced this fact squarely, he would have been aware that he was already living in a kind of pluralism. So was everyone, but the condition should have been even more evident to the Christian than to others.

There were certainly very real reasons for medieval man's attitude toward coexistence—or rather for his lack of a very positive attitude. The underdeveloped state of communications was one. The absence of a habit of thinking in quantitative terms was another. When we today think of the coexistence of thirteenth-century Christendom and heathendom, we almost automatically think of so many millions of persons here and so many there. (In preparation for this essay, at one point I began a search for such figures. The use of exact figures proved irrelevant almost immediately, but not until after I had thought seriously of using them.) Earlier man had no effective way of measuring large quantities of men. The first steps in modern demography were taken only toward the end of the Renaissance era.

In the total absence not only of reliable statistics but even of a general inclination to think in terms of statistics, not only about mankind but about reality generally, men all over the earth could not until the past few hundred years effectively imagine the multitudes of men outside their own immediate ken. While knowledge of what lay outside Christendom existed, it was so vague and so scattered that we can truly say that Christian theologians did not neglect the problem of mankind out-

side Christendom so much as they simply failed to
be struck by the problem.

But to note the real obstacles, psychological and
physical, to contact with other human beings felt
on the one side by Christendom and by the Judaism to which it is so mysteriously related, and on
the other side by the non-Hebraic and non-Christian world, is only to note that human society had
not progressed to the point where the fact of pluralism, at least on a global scale, could be assessed
and its problems faced in a real way. In earlier
human existence, that is to say for most of the
time man has been on the earth, religious differences had rather definite geographical correlatives.
Since national sovereignty is defined largely in
geographic terms, nationalism and religion have
been almost inextricably interwoven in this framework. *Cuius regio, eius religio* was a principle
enunciated by Cicero with slightly different word-
ing as a commonplace in his age: *Sua cuique civi-
tati religio est, nostra nobis* (*Pro Flacco* 2.8)—
"Each commonwealth has its own religion, and
we have ours." The principle obtained from pre-
historic times until very recent years practically
everywhere—Jean Jacques Rousseau, Comte, and
others comment on its success in the ancient world
—and it still obtains in most regions of the world
with greater or lesser rigor. The temporal perspectives must be kept in evidence here: a principle
such as this which has apparently obtained for

some four hundred thousand years (a fairly firm figure for man's existence on the earth) is not going to be obliterated in a mere few hundred years without considerable difficulty.

When nowadays in most Western societies, and in a growing number of Eastern societies, religious differences have correlatives other than geographical and nationalistic, and the problem of coexistence and pluralism thereby moves into a new stage, we must not be surprised if it does not move as fast as some short-sighted persons might expect it to do. As societies interact more and more on one another without improved communications, issues become exceedingly complex. The Catholic Church, for example, finds herself engaged today with all sorts of civilizations simultaneously, working in a great many different time coordinates, from new industrial and semi-industrial civilizations to very old, retarded civilizations such as those in Papua, or, what is more difficult, with civilizations, such as those in Italy and other parts of Europe or in parts of Latin America, which are a mingling of highly industrial elements and elements from centuries-old folkways.

Still, it is helpful to remember that the most retarded civilization of today is hardly more retarded than all civilizations have been for most of man's life on the planet, for most of some 400,000 years. Not only now but since the original breakthrough a few thousand years ago, civilization has been advancing at a pace which by any realistic historical standards has been surprisingly rapid.

What I have said so far involves no new discoveries. It is intended, however, to encourage a special awareness. We gain perspective by realizing that in the Christian economy especially, but not exclusively, the problem of coexistence and pluralism is basically an old human problem, not a recent one. It has been with man from the beginning. If it has not appeared urgent until very recent times because of the dispersion of the human race in relatively isolated groups over the surface of the earth, we should remember that this dispersion is not a normal or durable human condition. In his writings on evolution and the "human phenomenon" Père Pierre Teilhard de Chardin, S.J., has made much of the fact that, although the infra-human evolutionary pattern is typically "bushy," fraying out into greater and greater differentiation, greater and greater separation and divergence, the pattern of evolution within the human sphere, which is ultimately the sphere dominated by mind, by intelligence, is, on the contrary, convergent.

Immediately after his appearance, it is true, man spreads out over the face of the earth and develops minor divergences, the sort we note as racial differences today, physical and cultural. But once man has pretty well occupied the surface of the globe and developed the kind of thinking which enables him to realize his larger social potentialities, a complementary pattern of convergence sets in, a pattern which continuously accelerates its own development. Despite iron and bamboo curtains, and our own often blameworthy reluctance to share what we know with others (comparable to their blameworthy reluctance to share what they know with us), man is in still more contact with man today than at any other period in the history of our globe. The age of geographical races, as the distinguished racial anthropologist Carleton Coon has said, is *passé*. The former disseverance and divergence of the one human race, like human ignorance itself, was not a durable human condition. Man is made to unite humanity.

A corollary is that any society, past or present, insofar as it seals itself off from other human societies, is an inhuman society. It may have, or it may have had, reasons for doing so. But these reasons must, as soon as possible, be done away with. Man is made to deal with other men, not with only a certain group of men, and human society as a whole is cohesive. Because of this fact—not to mention the further fact that, at least for a Christian, all human beings must be the objects of a love and solicitude which presuppose and go far beyond the natural demands of humanity—the medieval types and other primitive types of coexistence by isolation, with their consequent pluralisms based on geographical divisions, are no longer acceptable. At best they have been tolerable for want of something better. But they are not a permanent condition; rather, they are full of tensions, fuller, in the long run, than our conditions in pluralistic societies today. The very lack of effective communications which lent plausibility to isolationism was a temporary condition, destined to be liquidated because of the very nature of man.

II

The breakthrough in geographical frontiers which has moved the question of coexistence into a new stage and made urgent the problems of pluralistic society has been marked not only by cataclysmic developments in communications which are forcing us to rethink our whole notion of human existence on our planet but also by a concomitant tendency of the communications process to work its way into man's mind as a frame of reference for his thinking about the universe and all being as well as about thought itself.

A cardinal point in this development within the past century and a half has been Hegel and the importance which he gives to dialectic. The notion of dialectic was old when Hegel laid hold of it, but with him it became urgent. However, the connection of dialectic with communication and in particular with real dialogue, the speaking of man to man, does not mean much to Hegel, and he could neither forecast nor foresee the stress on dialogue itself which marks our day and which leads Jaspers to state that "Communication is the path to truth in all its forms." Yet in looking back, we can see that the veering of interest from nature philosophies to a dialectical philosophy is a noteworthy manifestation of a shift toward Jaspers' outlook. Other developments in Hegel's day foreshadowed our present interest in communication: the spread of literacy and the imminent development of the telegraph and of the other instruments serving communication which followed the telegraph in such short order: the telephone, wireless, television, radar, and radio telescope, as well as the various forms of rapid transit, from the steam locomotive to the jet plane.

Whatever the interrelations of these phenomena, the age which has emerged and in which we live can reasonably be styled the communications age. At least, this is the American's way of looking at it. The European would be more inclined to view it as the age of dialogue. But the two come to much the same thing, although they register typical national differences in outlook. For, whether we call it the age of communication or of dialogue, ours is certainly the age which has become explicitly conscious of the importance of man's sharing his thoughts with others, the age in which millions of persons are set aside to expedite this sharing and in which the influence of this sharing, and its absolute necessity, are increasingly matters of prime interest to the philosopher and theologian, just as much as they are to the manufacturer and marketing expert.

Although geographical boundaries are of course still far from being annihilated, the simple expedient of sealing off the frontier can never again be serviceable in solving human problems to the extent to which it was in an earlier age. We must not lose sight of the fact that this is what the earlier sealing off of the frontier was—a means of solving problems of human relations. The economic and military and social ramifications of isolationist politics may be very real. But they are all mere fronts for the basic problem of isolationism: the problems of man's personal relations with his fellow man. Today we have reached the point where we can realize more clearly that geographical isolation settled nothing, for it is inevitably a temporary measure, doomed by the very nature of man and of human society. The experiment which resulted in the foundation of Liberia in 1822 is unthinkable in 1958: white and Negro Americans are going to have to talk the situation out and improve their personal relations right here.

The earlier attempts to resolve essentially human problems by geographical manipulation are connected with a reliance on diagrammatic analysis of essentially human problems which no longer seems real to thinking men. No spatial framework, however elaborate, can deal adequately with the relationship of person to person which is the ground of all human activity. When we seek something in the sensorium in terms of which we can deal with person-to-person relationships, we find that we must deal with them in terms of voice and speech and, ultimately, of sound.

This is the way in which I now propose to discuss the relationship between church and state as this affects religion in a free society in terms of dialogue, of voice, of speech between man and man. This is not exactly the same as to view them in terms of dialectic, Hegelian or other. Dialectic is, indeed, related to dialogue, for it is from dialogue between persons that the notion of dialectic is in one way or another derived. Nevertheless, dialectic is in philosophical discussion often given a formalistic, diagrammatic cast which we wish to avoid here. The three stages ordinarily associated with the Hegelian dialectic exhibit this diagrammatic or spatialized frame of mind: thesis (a "putting"), antithesis (a "putting against"), and synthesis (a "putting together"). I wish to cut back of such formalisms to the reality of a discussion or dialogue which establishes and develops relations between persons and to regard the church-state relationship and the religious-secular relationship by analogy with a discussion between persons.

New Testament prescriptions concerning the relationships between church and state or religion and secular culture have little of the spatial or diagrammatic about them. There is nothing like the prescription purported to be enshrined in the long Indian name for the Connecticut lake which means "You-fish-on-your-side-I-fish-on-my-side-nobody-fish-in-the-middle." There is nothing said of "territory" or "areas" of sovereignty. But there is reference to persons. Thus Jesus replies to his questioners, "Render to Caesar the things that are Caesar's, and to God the things that are God's" (Matthew xxii 21). Here is the state personalized in Caesar and contrasted with a personal God. To Pilate, Jesus says, "I am a king," but "My kingdom is not of this world" (John xviii 36-37). Here the Kingdom is His own personal rule. Paul's familiar dialectical relationships, those between Jew and gentile (or Jew and Greek), converted gentile and unconverted Jew, converted Jew and unconverted gentile (Romans xi 7-23), bond servant and free-man, male and female (Galatians iii 28), are all presented basically not as relationships between abstract ideas but as dialogic relationships between persons. The same type of relationships govern St. Augustine's City of God and City of Man, or St. Ignatius Loyola's Standard of Christ and Standard of Lucifer; these, too, are relationships based on person-to-person oppositions.

This personal quality of dialogue is the first of the qualities relevant to the notion as it affects our present subject. The relationship of church and state to one another, or of the religious and secular to one another shows its personalist roots in various ways. For one thing, it is the relationship of two things not entirely manageable in terms of abstract ideas. It did not originate in abstraction and it cannot end there.

In its present form, the church-state tension came into being in the Roman empire, when men personally committed to a personal God (in the tradition which the Christians shared with the Hebrews) stated: "We may not and will not worship the Roman gods, although we will be loyal to the Roman rule, and that because of the demands of the same faith which keeps us from worshiping the Roman gods." This stand jolted pagan society, which had presumed that one changed his religious stand according to political necessity, as one changed his civil position. But Christians were ready to die rather than change, as Hebrews had been before them, although the theocratic nature of Hebrew civil society seemingly precluded the loyalty to a pagan state which the Christians, following Pauline teaching (Ephesians vi 5), felt obligatory.

It was this stand which precipitated, and still precipitates, disputations about the tensions between church and state. The disputations did not precipitate the stand, but vice versa. The Christian stand precipitated theories about the separation of church and state.

The church-state tension is personal also in the sense that it is lived within the souls of individual persons. It is a tension which calls for constant individual action and decision on the part of those religiously committed. For the tension is one which can never be liquidated by formulas but one to be lived through and with. This is not to say that formulas are irrelevant or unserviceable or untrue—to say this would be to belie the full tension of the situation. They are, or can be, very relevant and serviceable and true, but they are never complete when brought to bear on a concrete situation, where decision must always take into account matters which are unformulated.

Further, the church-state tension is personal because of the communal nature of the church. In *Man's Western Quest,* Denis de Rougemont has pointed out the difference between the Jewish and Christian sense of communal worship and the worship in isolation found in other religions. The Christian notion of the church is adumbrated by the Hebrew notion of the people of God. Various Christians feel the communal notion of the church variously, but they all feel it to some degree. In the Catholic Church it is so strong that the central act of worship, the sacrifice of the Mass, is always and inevitably an act of the entire Church, even though the faithful may not be in attendance. (It is to be noted that it is forbidden for a priest, without special authorization, to celebrate Mass with no one else in attendance.) Indeed, since all Catholics' prayers are referable to this Great Prayer, there is a sense in which no Catholic's prayer can be entirely private. His prayer is always with the community.

If its personal cast is the first dialogic quality

of the church-state, religious-secular relationship, a second, and related, quality is its sense of direction combined with a lack of conclusiveness. Dialogue itself as such has purpose, but it has no particular terminus. Since the resources of personal give-and-take on which it draws are bottomless, a dialogue can always proceed further. Not only that, but it should proceed further if the lives of persons are to continue. This does not mean that it is incessant, but that, while it may be quiescent at any given moment, it is always alive and capable of further growth. Because the dialogue between church and state or between the religious and the secular is—in an analogous way, of course, but really—like the dialogue between persons, it cannot possibly be frozen off or entirely repressed. Persons may be distinguishable one from the other, but they prove their very distinctness by contact with those who are not themselves.

The Church herself needs to be *in* the world just as desperately as she needs not to be *of* it. And the state cannot with impunity pretend that religion, or anything else which exists, is nonexistent.

The personal and inconclusive quality of the religious-secular relationship when thought of as a dialogue makes it a particularly painful reality to persons of a certain cast of mind which we might style visualist. If the City of God is related to the City of Man dialogically, we shall have to face the fact honestly that the two Cities cannot be thought of as related to one another by means of any neat spatial model.

We cannot in any satisfactory way imagine the state as existing on one side of a kind of lot and the church or churches on another side, with or without a wall of separation between them. To do so is to fall into a trap especially designed for himself and others by the sixteenth century savant Peter Ramus. Anxious to distinguish the various "arts" from one another and particularly rhetoric from logic, Ramus had recourse to this sort of suburban development scheming in things of the mind. From the legislation of Greek antiquity he dredged up what he called "Solon's Law," which had prescribed in ancient Athens that alongside each wall be left a clear space of one foot, alongside each house a clear space of two feet, and so on. With the "constant undaunted resolution of maintaining his own Opinions" which Hobbes was later to share, Ramus persuaded himself and thousands upon thousands of followers that somehow or other there was an exact correspondence between the real estate situation in ancient Athens and the condition of logic and rhetoric in sixteenth-century Europe. Rhetoric and logic—and indeed all the arts—were to be kept clear of one another in teaching by at least a foot or two all the way around. Unfortunately for Ramus, knowledge does not really exist in "zones," so that it became difficult, if not impossible, to know what his buffer zone of a foot or two around logic or rhetoric could in fact possibly mean.

Even so, Ramus seemingly had more confidence in human nature than some recent legalists have had. He was content with a vacated buffer zone, an intellectual no-man's-land of very scant depth, to separate the areas of knowledge as he envisioned them. More recently, resorting to the same diagrammatic approach to church-state relationships, and under the influence of the visualist eighteenth-century thinking retailed to us by Thomas Jefferson, but suspicious of mere empty space, we have sought to erect a "wall of separation" on the border between religious and secular culture.

But, whatever honest progress we may have made in our thinking, the wall has not helped much. For there is no satisfactory way of conceiving the reality of the church (or of secular activity) as occupying two different plots of ground. "Good fences make good neighbors," Robert Frost reminds us. But how to consider religious activity and secular activity even as next-door neighbors when both are my own? The concepts are not related to one another in a very effective next-door way. When we are considering the religious-secular situation in terms of dialogue we are considering it in a way which cannot be reduced to such visual models, no matter how elaborate such models may be made.

Its resistance to visualist formulation, which is to say "clear" formulation, is a third quality of the religious-secular situation. It is not simply that the dialogic situation is a moving one rather than a static one—although this is of some relevance, for the visualist mind is impatient until it has reduced all to quiescence, at least in the sense in which actual movement can be made static by being committed to an immobile drawing or chart or set of figures. The dialogue situation is more than moving. It is moving in a way which does not yield to diagramming, which cannot be adequately pictured or reduced entirely to "form."

The reason for this is that the movement of dialogue—and the religious-secular relationship insofar as it is like this movement—is essentially a movement concerned with an "I" and a "thou," and not with "objects." And there is no way for me to picture the intimate and incommunicable self which I sense is you (or "thou"). I can express this self of mine by the mental and the spoken word "I" only by reason of the fact that I utter the word "I" —for this word means something decidedly different to me than it does to you or to anyone else who uses it. And I can express your self by "you" or "thou" only by addressing myself *to* you. For, although "you" or "thou" means something quite different to every single one of the thousands of persons to whom I may speak it, it can be given definition and individual application within a real dialogue and only within a real dialogue. "You" means the person to whom I am actually addressing myself and for whom, and *while I address him,* I can use no name, no *nomen,* no noun, but only this curious thing which we designate as a *pronomen* or pronoun, a substitute name. Unlike a real noun or name, the pronoun "thou" must be assigned its role, its reference, in terms of a going dialogue and in no other way. It signifies in terms of a personal sharing in every instance unique because it is between two unique persons. Of such a sharing I can form no picture and certainly no adequate diagram.

This "I" and "thou" are of course known in a situation which itself engages the object world, for although "I" and "thou" are not objects but persons, they become known to one another only through dealings in terms of objects. I become aware of myself and of you as I talk *to* you *about* things. But by the same token, objects themselves become known to us only in a dialogue situation, as we talk to another, or listen to another talking, about them.

Dialogue is thus moving, and lends motion to other things, not in the sense that it makes certainty about objects impossible, for it leads to many objective certainties (although not to certainty in everything), but in the sense that it is open to the continued and limitless influence of one person on another. Through dialogue, one person does not seek to annihilate the other (although Sartre would try to have it this way, and perhaps

Hegel's dialectic of master and slave would, too), nor even to understand another in the sense in which one understands an object, by "grasping" it. There is no way for one person to "grasp" another as he might "grasp" a mathematical theorem or a principle of economics. The "hold" which one person has on another is better called "appeal," which is to say a kind of "calling" (*appellare* means "to call"), and such appeal comes into being through love. By dialogue a person seeks not to grasp but to commune, to open himself to another and to enter into the other who has reciprocally opened his mind and heart to him.

For human beings, dialogue is thus developmental. It develops the persons who take part in it, enabling them to realize to a greater extent their own promise and perfections. Indeed, from one point of view the whole of human life is simply a dialogue with other men and with God. In the quality of the dialogue to which it has contributed the measure of each human life can be taken.

III

Because the church-state or religious-secular relationship thus ultimately resists complete and total formulation does not mean that it is unintelligible or that it cannot be dealt with. We must attempt all the limited formulations which are true and possible. But while we realize their truth, we must also realize their limitations, acknowledging that the problems here are not grounded in the relationship of object to object, of thing to thing, but in the commitment of person to person.

To think of religious-secular relationships in a dialogic rather than a diagrammatic fashion is thus to acknowledge their connections with the human person, for dialogue serves the needs of the human person. Here it will be helpful to consider some of the ways in which the church and the state, or the religious and the secular, affect the world of human persons as such.

In the West at least, the state has certainly progressed more and more toward respect for the individual person. The ancient Greek or Roman state, supported directly on slavery, is superseded by the medieval European state in which, although some slavery certainly existed, most slavery had been mitigated to serfdom, and the so-called servile arts by which most persons subsisted were accorded a respect unknown among most peoples in ancient times. Such a society is succeeded by a somewhat piratical age of enlightened free enterprise in which, if millions of persons are repressed, a tremendous resentment builds up throughout society against their repression until we arrive at the social legislation which is a commonplace in our day. Conditions today are far from perfect, and yet this over-all pattern of development is certainly one which acknowledges the responsibility of secular society as a whole and, where necessary, of the state itself to make possible the personal development of each and every individual.

At the same time, however, that this respect for the individual human person is in many ways building up, the state itself is increasingly depersonalized. Part of this growth in depersonalization comes from mere growth in size. Personal contact between those in Washington and 170,000,000 individual citizens over the United States is less feasible than it was between the leader of an Anglo-Saxon *comitatus* and his small group of followers.

But there seems to be a necessary movement toward depersonalization in the evolution of government. Growth in size itself is not an accident, but necessary and intrinsic to the pattern of the evolution of human society as man fulfills his role of taking over the earth. Moreover, the very notion of justice to which the state is committed has something impersonal about it. For the personal God of Jews and Christians, His mercy, not His justice, is above all His works. In secular society, however, after a certain time kingship appears doomed, and with it the notion of government as a personal perogative to which one is born which kingship epitomizes. Its doom is effected, not by any accident but by the very shape which human affairs as a whole are taking, for kings, and their satellite nobility, perish not in isolation but directly as a functioning class.

It is false, of course, to assume that the state is ever completely depersonalized. As Dr. Martin Buber has pointed out, even the most complexly bureaucratic structures of contemporary society are still made up of persons and of personal decisions. Nevertheless, the time arrives when it is no longer possible to equate the state in the West with a person. "L'Etat c'est moi" becomes an anachronism.

What happens in the state happens in a parallel fashion in secular life generally, as the smaller, personalized units of activity are absorbed—never entirely, but to a great extent—in the larger, more systematized units which mark our age. As organization moves in, the personal to some extent suffers. For, as Buber again has pointed out, the "I" and the "thou" cannot be organized; only the "it" can be.

And yet, since it is persons who in the last analysis effect organization, it is not surprising that under these conditions men immediately devise compensations for the depersonalizing momentum which organization can develop, and devise the compensations *within* organization itself. At one level, and a low one, there is the "personal touch," the gift which is made by a machine and then "personalized" by having something added to it which had been made by another machine, but which somehow allows one's good intentions to show. At a slightly higher level, there is the personnel director, the personnel consultant, and the counselors who haunt the peripheries of our lives. At a still higher level, men in our day have worked out a personalist philosophy, a philosophy of the "I" and the "thou," thereby making the age which in one way has depersonalized itself into the age more conscious of the human person than any age before. I do not mean that everywhere today the human person is honored more than before: but in the over-all pattern of human society, I believe the person is.

Three things should be noted in connection with the emergence of a militantly personalist philosophy. First, this philosophy did not emerge until there were a large number of persons on earth— the very antithesis of mass and person helped make evident the sacredness and uniquenes of the person as never before. In earlier ages, men had found comfort in vaunting their minds or their powers of speech over the powers of nature, thereby assuring themselves of their own excellence. There was little time or effort or interest left over to assure the human individual of his own importance. He was left to assume this importance—often against terrible odds, in the face of facts which controverted it on every hand. With the evidence of man's mastery over vast areas of nature (not by any means all areas) he has had time to think through his own value, as well as his dependence, *vis-à-vis* his fellow man—his dependence, for sociology, too, is a product of the modern age (if not so recent a one as a personalist philosophy).

This brings us to the second point, namely, that the personalist outlook is dependent upon a high degree of organization in human society—organization of the "it," if you will, but organization which it is not wise to belittle or scorn. Of course, a personalist philosophy is itself a kind of organization and as such is not the same as what we might call a "going" "I"-"thou" relationship, but I believe no one would maintain that it has nothing to do with such a relationship.

The third thing to note in connection with the emergence of a militantly personalist philosophy is this: even though it may be considered with other philosophies as in certain ways a secular enterprise, such a philosophy tends to develop almost immediately religious overtones. Aristotelian nature philosophy can be concerned with God, but it is with a kind of thing-God who, as Aristotle with some plausibility maintained, was quite unconcerned with the doings of anything below Himself. This approach to the divine is a kind of polar opposite to real religious practice. A personalist philosophy, whether in Kierkegaard, M. Gabriel Marcel, or Dr. Buber is not so distant from religious reality. It turns on personal commitment.

It thus appears that social organization has generated as one of the correctives for its own depersonalizing tendencies certain movements which rise toward the religious. We can next turn to the question of religion itself, asking how personal the sphere of religion and of the church is as compared with that of the state. I shall here center my attention on the Catholic Church and the Catholic religion for the reason that I can speak from the fullest acquaintanceship and experience here, although I shall try not to exclude other religions or religious views, bringing these in where I can, at least by inference, and allowing you to fill out or correct my remarks with your own knowledge and experience.

By every test it would seem that in the dialogue between the secular and the religious, it is the latter which speaks with the more personal voice, at least within the Hebraeo-Christian tradition. In a remarkable chapter in his remarkable book *Mimesis,* the late Erich Auerbach makes a point about the difference between the literature of the Greeks and the Old Testament by adverting to the opening of the twenty-second chapter of Genesis: "And it came to pass after these things that God did tempt Abraham, and said to him, Abraham! and he said, here I am." Nowhere in Greek literature, explains Auerbach, can such a passage be matched. Homer portrays his heroes rather exhaustively, so that the reader has virtually no questions to ask about their personal histories when Homer is finished. But the Biblical characters, both God and Abraham, burst onto the scene as persons thrust themselves into our lives, immediately but also mysteriously, for, as real persons, they act from motives which are not entirely clear to the onlooker and which lead us back into the mysterious depths of the individual personality with its own individual and bottomless history.

This personal setting for the contact between God and man is essential to the Hebraic and to the Christian tradition, and without it the Bible, Old Testament and New Testament, is quite meaningless. This personal contact exists under all organization or "structure" in Hebraic and Christian tradition, and gives organization or structure its necessity and its meaning and its role.

When we look in the Hebrew and Christian tradition for what distinguishes the sacred from the secular, we find that the sacred is somehow governed by the individual conscience *vis-à-vis* its God. Here is the realm of real love and of real sin—not of feelings of guilt which the psychiatrist must handle, but of defection from what should be the object of personal love. A conscience which is formed solely on abstract principles, if such a conscience is possible, without reference to a personal God is, from a Christian point of view, a secular conscience.

The Catholic is of course committed to his religious position by reason of his conscience: defection from it would be for him defection from a personal commitment and obligation to a personal God. His attitude toward the visible Church is governed by this interior commitment. For this Church is not a mere "organization" but a mysterious extension of the Person of Christ, Who is Himself God. It is the Mystical Body of Christ.

Because of the interiority of the human person which she acknowledges and respects, the Catholic Church in her own laws makes explicit allowance for a division which the civil law does not know: that between the external forum, which concerns the law as it is a basis for the Church's public judgments, and the internal forum, which concerns the law as it relates to a person's own interior conscience. A person who has violated a law publicly in the external forum and incurs some sort of censure for this violation may, in the internal forum, be in quite good standing.

For example, to be excommunicated a Catholic must have done something wrong which is morally imputable to him—an excommunication cannot be attached to any other kind of action. Let us take a case of an act to which an excommunication is attached—for example, a man's entering that section of the convent of nuns which is "cloistered," that is, which is set aside as the living quarters of the nuns and from which he is excluded—and suppose that such an act is performed out of inadvertence or simple ignorance of the law. Since no real sin is committed, no excommunication is incurred. Although in the external forum his excommunication would be presumed by those who knew of the external act, he would not really have been excommunicated in the internal forum, which is to say, as far as his conscience goes. Ordinarily the internal forum and the external correspond, but when they do not, it is the *internal* which the Church herself in her *externally* promulgated laws explicitly recognizes as the more important.

For this reason, that is, the Church's persistent concern with the individual's conscience above all externalities, the external organization of the Catholic Church appears in constant danger of crumbling. The "it" of her laws is always yielding to the "I"-"thou" relationship of their application. Where the Church most closely touches the individual conscience, in the confessional, the relationship is strictly man-to-man, so much so that the Church can demand to know nothing whatsoever about the state of the individual conscience there revealed, or about the action which her minister, the priest, has taken with regard to it.

The priest himself is obliged in conscience to follow God's law and the Church's law—in itself impersonal, for its function is to make it impossible for one man to dominate over another simply as a person. Yet his application of the law is made in a real dialogic situation between persons which is inviolate.

The confessor is the public minister of the Church and of God's pardon, but his public role is so private that—short of the penitent's special permission to do so—he can never say anything to anyone else in the Church or out, which would reveal the failings which the penitent has disclosed to him. At this focal point of the public administration of the Church, what is public and external, and controlled by public and external laws, is swallowed up in privacy, a privacy which is constituted by a judicial dialogue. Nothing quite like this is thinkable in secular law because of the less personal setting of the secular.

The intimacy which governs even the external ministrations of the Church and gives them their highly personal cast makes it understandable why the principal treatment of the Church in the writings of St. Thomas Aquinas occurs not in the *Summa Theologiae,* but in his *Explanation of the Canticle of Canticles.* The intimacy and love are at the root of the Church's being, but, as the body is very much in evidence in Canticles, so the Church has her body, too. Indeed, the Church is, in Catholic teaching, not simply an organization but a mysterious extension of the Person of Christ Himself: the Church is His "Mystical Body," involving the persons within her fold in His personal destiny in history.

It is not without good reason that in his book mentioned above, *Man's Western Quest,* Denis de Rougemont, convinced that man's Western quest has been the appreciation of the value of the human person, has traced the urgent concern with the person in the West back to the first three ecumenical councils of Nice, Constantinople, and Ephesus. Here, where the Church as an organism is battling through the capital questions of the consubstantiality of the Father and the Son, the divinity of the Holy Spirit, and the unity of the

Person in Christ, we find the seeds of this concern with the person which has grown ever since. It would be untrue to say that all concern with person traces to a source in revelation. The term *persona* arose in Greek secular culture and was taken over by Christians. But within the Christian economy the notion has received its plenary development. Even Dr. Buber's personalism is by no means a purely Jewish development. It is the product of a fine Jewish mind operating under strong Christian influences.

The foregoing instances serve merely as samples of the personalism one finds rooted in religion in the Hebraic and Christian tradition, even where this tradition manifests most clearly its organizational aspects. In this connection, too, we should not fail to note one important fact: although a person is precisely that utter interiority and simplicity to which the concept of "organization" can hardly be applied, it is precisely the so-called "organized" religions which have kept most alive the sense of a personal God. When in the Jewish and Christian tradition strict religious "organization" has been depreciated in favor of purely personal religion or loosely-held-together ethical societies, by an apparently inescapable momentum God begins to be assimilated to some impersonal "force." There may be some exception to this theorem, but the over-all pattern is unmistakable.

The strangely personalizing function of strictly religious organization in the Hebraic and Christian tradition is highly important, for it shows that organization in the Church and organization in the state are in reality quite different things. The concept of "power" associated with "organization" and "institutionalization" is at best a very difficult concept to use in a meaningful way with regard to human society and activity. To use the concept indiscriminately for religious organization and for secular organization, conceiving of these as opposed to one another in the way in which two taps on a common source of energy might be, is to dissociate oneself from actuality and to retreat into the unresolved conflicts of one's own subconscious.

As we have seen, the organization of the state moves away from a stress on a central or governing person to a kind of impersonality. It cannot avoid doing this, for its organization is concerned precisely with what is exterior about man: at least in the American tradition the state carefully dissociates itself from the personal life and choices of the individual so far as it can. It can never do so entirely, but it can come close to approximating a neutrality here.

Here the problem of commitment of the individual to the state arises. Loyalty or commitment has a high personal valence. It demands a personal setting in which to grow and become real. To what can loyalty or commitment be directed in the case of a depersonalized state?

It is common to maintain that persons are loyal to an "idea" or to an "ideal." But really to determine such an ideal, to give it definition, to formulate it, to assign it content is often not an easy thing to do. Some recent political studies have shown—as though we were not aware already—how often voting is influenced not by the ideals professed by one or another political party but by the symbolic appeal of the persons for or against whom one votes.

The difficulty of formulating the notion of democracy in a way satisfactory to all who profess devotion to it is well known. This difficulty is not peculiar to democracy. Communism, which professes to be a more complete, and indeed an exhaustive, political ideology, exercises its real large-scale appeal through the persons of leaders who are accorded a secular form of canonization suggesting the politico-religious canonization of the emperors of ancient Rome.

Throughout the political order we note this tendency to substitute for ideals, which are supposed to furnish operative goals, persons who really make possible the personal commitment of others. For persons need no determination or definition or formulation. They are there, given realities—mysterious and impenetrable, but for all that the most real things we know. It is their reality which makes our commitment possible. For commitment is a form of love, and what we must love in the last analysis is not ideas or ideals but a person, a "thou" which provides the resonance which our person requires.

I do not call attention to the depersonalizing momentum in the modern state because of any belief that such a momentum is not good. It would seem that it is good, and that it is normal for a state, while learning to respect more and more individual human persons, to become itself more and more impersonal in its administrative aspects. I do not at all believe that a regression toward feudalism or other systems of personalized, and somewhat whimsical administration would be desirable. But there is a danger in the case of the modern state, a danger of self-deception on the part of the citizenry. Since the state as such is in great part depersonalized, and since our own drives and personal commitments, when they are most urgent and most effective, are inextricably involved in persons, we can deceive ourselves into thinking that our commitments and actions stand on grounds more abstract than is the case. More often they are to groups of real persons, invested perhaps with more or less symbolic reference to other persons outside for immediate purview. We need to be aware of the personal ground of many of our supposedly impersonal secular commitments, and to the fact that our loyalty in a democracy is in some way or other, actually a commitment to all of the millions of persons who make up our democratic society much more than it is loyalty to any "principles."

In handling the problem of church-state or religious-secular relationships today in American society, it would seem that we should pay more attention to personal relationships, of which in many ways democratic society is becoming increasingly conscious. Society is a curious whole of which the parts—human persons—are also wholes. A democracy is a society which respects the wholeness of the persons of which it is composed and which derives its special strength from their wholeness. It is a society thus destined to live in a constant state of tension.

There is thus a sense in which democracy encourages love, for commitment is a form of love. This is not to say, however, that democracy is evangelical, that it performs the same role as religion, that it belongs to the City of God. It is only to say that what develops in a democracy can serve the purposes of the City of God. God's kingdom is one of grace, and supernatural charity is more than the civil love which a citizen has for all his fellow citizens. Yet this love is more congenial to God's kingdom than hate would be.

Dialogue has been our focus here because it is a way of achieving unity while preserving difference—the basic difference between one person and another. Here at the close it can also command our attention as a therapeutic.

In this world persons do live under the constant threat of war, not only between nations but between individuals themselves. Institutions, such as democracies, which encourage persons to develop themselves become involved in this same threat.

A democracy may perish in the cataclysm when its citizens come to blows. In the face of this threat dialogue within a democracy does not guarantee peace, but it promotes it.

Dialogue is an action whereby an individual asserts—and even in the first instance discovers—his own uniqueness by the very process of uniting himself with another or others. The prelude to war is to halt dialogue, to cease to talk, to break off diplomatic relations. So long as we continue talking to one another, we cannot be entirely hostile. Our dialogue should, moreover, look not only or chiefly to establishing points of disagreement, although it may have to do this. It must find points of agreement, too.

All communication, all dialogue, has this effect: it unites, and this despite the greatest difference there is, that between your person and mine, between you and me. But, finally, dialogue must be between persons who are fully persons by being committed, by having taken a stand in the world of persons. Otherwise it will degenerate into the mere talk of a television commercial. In the tension between personal commitment and a love, not for humanity but for all individual men, the promise of a free society will best be realized.

2

CENSORSHIP IN
A DIALECTICAL REPUBLIC

Stringfellow Barr

I

It would seem that, in a free society, the most crucial case of conflict between church and state is censorship. There are, for example, the cases in which religiously organized groups, in order to protect faith or morals, attempt to secure legislation that would prevent the teaching of a false doctrine—let us say Marxism. There are the cases where such groups intimidate local officials into stretching the law: thwarting free assembly in the interest of "public order" or preventing the sale of certain books or the acting of certain plays in the interest of "public morals." There is the use, on religious grounds, of blacklisting and boycott.

There is very little actual agreement in our society either on the moral justification for, or the constitutionality of, these types of censorship. On the whole, the First Amendment is treated as a pious declaration of an impossible goal; or as a traditional feature of our high standard of living, a luxury that can be dispensed with; or, at best, as a hard-won truce between inimical social groups, sick of such bloody struggles as the Religious Wars—a truce in which each of us regretfully allows his neighbor to say whatever comes into his foolish head on condition that he will allow us to speak the truth which we alone possess. The implication of this "tolerance" is that if our group were strong enough to silence other groups, we should all be the gainers. The First Amendment, if we read it this way, stabilized an earlier "balance of terror" and is fortified by growing indifference about the issues. Perhaps we analogize from our material possessions, our private property: I will help guarantee your title to your house if you will help guarantee my title to mine, although a more attractive condition of affairs would be for my title to be guaranteed and yours not. I will help guarantee your right to voice your opinions if you will help guarantee my right to voice mine. *Quid pro quo.*

On these grounds I find no very interesting principle to appeal to when confronted with a problem of censorship. But I think I can discern a principle if I analogize from public property, such as highways or harbors, instead of from private property —if, indeed, I consider the First Amendment as having been designed primarily to protect and promote the common good. This is why I find Plato's *Republic* so illuminating on censorship and, in our own generation, Alexander Meiklejohn's *Free Speech*. Meiklejohn points out that under our constitution the people are both the rulers and the ruled. As rulers, they cannot govern wisely unless they have complete access to both fact and opinion. It is this right of the electorate, in terms of their responsibilities, that basically undergirds the First Amendment. Any effort to screen what the voter may hear interferes with the governing function of a free society. This is why Meiklejohn considers Mr. Justice Holmes's free-speech decision with its formal qualification of a clear and present danger inadequate and worse. It is in effect a contradiction, saying that the Congress shall not abridge freedom of speech except where it judges it necessary to abridge it—and, of course, where the Court agrees. Meiklejohn prefers Mr. Justice Brandeis's insight: that so long as the physical means of exchanging ideas continue to exist, the presence of danger is no excuse for forbidding the exchange.

Meiklejohn is convinced that only the censorship which promotes such exchange can be justified, and he offers some handy examples of censorship that does just that. In parliamentary procedure, for instance, a man can very frequently be silenced by the chair: he hasn't got the floor. Or he can be ruled out of order for a variety of reasons; and, if he trespasses beyond certain limits, he can be thrown clear out of the meeting. All these things may happen in the effort to protect and promote a dialectical process—in this case, political deliberation. To abolish these rules of procedure in the name of freedom would clearly prove a doctrinaire, empty, Pyrrhic victory.

Examples of this sort of victory can be readily multiplied. The newspaper man cries freedom of the press when he is excluded from a diplomatic negotiation. The television man raises the same cry when a judge forbids his camera in the courtroom. In both cases censorship may promote the appropriate dialectic. A court trial is not secret because it is not televised; and a treaty is not secret because the process of negotiating it was. In each case the censorship channelizes the dialectic, but it does not prevent it.

It is, I think, only an apparent paradox that Plato should have stated this problem so clearly. Plato's republic, like Meiklejohn's, guarantees a continuous dialectic, a continuous exchange of ideas, between those who rule it. Indeed, Plato's republic, unlike our American republic today, follows special educational procedures in order that its rulers shall be capable of conducting good dialectic. Modern readers are usually horrified by Plato's rigorous censorship; but, quite clearly, the purpose of that censorship is to develop rulers who would not need it. It is true that in the Platonic republic only a fraction of the adults rule, and we modern democrats are shocked by this. But I want to suggest here, following Meiklejohn, that those who ultimately rule—with us, the electorate—must not be kept in the dark by censorship. With us, the electorate may properly "censor" what is available to minors, as the "guardians" of Plato's republic censored for their own non-rulers.

Plato's republic is, of course, a picture of an imaginary and ideal city-state. But I would insist that by ready extension it is a picture of the good society, the open society, the truly free society. I take it that what makes and keeps it open is its guarantee of the dialectical process. It guarantees that the community's problems shall be subjected to a continuous and joint examination. It guarantees that a certain kind of conversation shall never cease.

It is clear that for Plato this continuous dialectic was a human good, quite aside from its value to wise government. Like Aristotle, Plato knew that men are interdependent on two levels, not merely on one. For the health of their bodies, they need to exchange commodities; and they need the division of labor which Adam Smith so eloquently outlines in *The Wealth of Nations*. But, for the good of their minds, they need another division of labor and another exchange—the exchange of ideas. They need each other to help them learn. "All men," wrote Aristotle in that ringing first sentence of the *Metaphysics*, "all men by nature desire to know."

It is not only, therefore, that the common good requires good deliberation and that censorship must not becloud deliberation. It is that good theoretical speculation is also one of man's needs and that censorship endangers speculation, too. Indeed, Aristotle strongly implies that the highest function of government is to enable this joint speculation. I believe the First Amendment, when courageously adhered to, serves these necessities of man; serves free and responsible government; and even sets good political conditions for religious life. Of course, the good operation of the First Amendment depends on the good education of the electorate, and this to a degree that we Americans have not yet faced up to.

If my argument thus far is valid, then government must under no circumstances forbid "the preaching of false doctrines," whether that doctrine be religious, political, or economic. We all know there are many individuals and groups in our society who have not accepted this prohibition. Yet, even if the true doctrine which these groups long to protect by force be true, force is not its proper protection. Dialectic is. The trouble with protecting true doctrines by the sword and the stake is not merely that in a pluralistic society nobody possesses an adequate monopoly of stakes at which to burn infidels. The real trouble is that men, not being merely animals, but animals who by nature desire to know, cannot long be governed, as dogs are governed, by force—nor even by force and love. A human community lives in part by argument, by the word.

In the United States not many persons or groups would publicly advocate silencing opinions that are considered evil—except in desperate cases. An effective majority of Americans seems prepared to prevent the Communist from preaching his false doctrine and thereby subverting "the American way of life," and an effective majority of white Southerners seems prepared to prevent the integrationist from preaching his "false" doctrine and thereby subverting what is increasingly called "the Southern way of life." But no group seems prepared to submit all opinions, or even most opinions, to censorship. In principle, we accept freedom of speech where doctrines and opinions are concerned. But our anti-intellectual distrust of the power of truth makes us add: "Except, of course, in the case of—."

If the dialectical process really is necessary to the common good, then what shall we say of persons or groups who seem to withdraw from it? Are they traitors to the common good? What about a Thoreau? What about a religious group like, for instance, the Roman Catholic hierarchy? Do they not, by at least theoretically closing certain prohibited books to the laity in their charge, prevent these Catholic lay citizens of our common republic from participating in the common dialectic? There is indeed this possibility, if not in practice with Catholics, then in the case of a voluntary religious association which one could readily imagine.

I suggest that the risks of withdrawal either by individuals or groups must be accepted. Not merely because of Mr. Justice Douglas's moving statement that the right to privacy is the basis of all our liberties, but explicitly because Thoreau and the Catholic laity may be helping the dialectic more by their apparent withdrawal from it than if they were right in there pitching. We Americans should restrain our activist tendency to denounce those individuals who stand silent on a bank at Walden and those groups of individuals— those minorities, as we say—who may be carrying on their own dialectic and reaching a position that will later contribute in crucial fashion to the dialectic of the whole community.

II

Would the same hold good for religious "pressure groups"? Not if the term means a group that tries to gain its end—say, the censoring of certain films or the silencing of certain "subversives" by the manipulation of power rather than by the persuasion of reason. The fact that such groups may have higher aims than the oil lobby scarcely seems to excuse them. It is doubtful how well the means of oil lobbies can serve the ends of religion. It is this mesalliance that has aroused much of the public anger against censorship by church groups, just as the mesalliance of the Crusades between the Cross and its non-violence on the one hand and the pillage and raping of armies on the other hand aroused much of the Middle East's hatred of Christianity. Is this why our later "crusades" against vice so often backfire?

It may be that Plato's distinction between dialectic and eristic will best illuminate these pressure-groups-for-high-moral-ends. Plato points out that eristic is argument for the sake of winning and tends to be conducted with no holds barred. It substitutes the violence of sophistry for the violence of physical struggle. Stated more simply, its means are fraud, not force. To the uninitiated it sounds like dialectic.

But it is not dialectic. In genuine dialectic, the purpose of each side is to learn, not to win. In genuine dialectic, one may be genuinely grateful for "losing a point"—because one has lost a false opinion along with it.

I do not believe it is romantic to say that although there will perhaps always be plenty of eristic at the level of political action, as Plato so well knew, yet this political eristic will be more tinged with dialectic in a politically mature society than in a politically immature one. A few years ago when the reckless smear increased in use and the discussion of issues decreased, we Americans were merely being more immature politically than usual.

Those who expect to abolish government by pressure group are no doubt naive Utopians. The only persons more naive are those who joyfully accept the pressure group as a substitute for genuine debate of issues. It is naive to expect at any time soon to eliminate eristic. It is a lie in the soul to mistake eristic for dialectic. And when groups, acting in the name of morality and religion, try by fast political footwork and the manipulation of bloc votes to save the nation's morals, is it not possible that they are unintentionally clowning?

However, even like Plato, we are troubled by "the poets," not only the poets in the usual narrow sense, but the novelists, the dramatists, the painters, the sculptors, the musicians. We are frightened by so-called works of imagination and by the extraordinary power they exercise over men to ennoble or debase. Nearly all of us draw the line at some degree of indecency, obscenity, pornography —"immorality," as the Victorians modestly put it. We may not agree with the sexually repressed spinster or patrioteer or semi-literate judge who presumes to decide for us whether James Joyce or D. H. Lawrence is mere filth, not to be lawfully offered for sale. But we think that if the problem of obscene books, plays, and movies were left to qualified persons, then censorship would be justified. We sometimes add that, fortunately, the dialectic will not be affected, since that has to do with opinions and propositions, not with aesthetic perceptions.

But is this true? The history of literature, like the history of painting, offers strong evidence of a continuous dialectic—a dialectic carried on in images, in images that directly mirror ideas. And is it not likely that the health and sanity of a community depend not only on the dialectic of opinion but on the dialectic of the image: that is, on a lively movement in the arts? Unless this aesthetic dialectic feeds and nourishes the dialectic of proposition, of speculation, of deliberation, the latter appears to degenerate into empty verbalization. Other things being equal, therefore, we ought to hold the aesthetic dialectic also free from the censor. We should stop using force, not merely against what an unqualified pressure group thinks is obscene, but against what really is.

There are, our friends will tell us, some so-called works of art whose obvious and sole purpose is to arouse sexual desire. Surely these should not be allowed. But there may be a difficulty here. I assume that censorship is not being urged on us as the means of punishing the vicious intentions of certain artists, but to prevent certain effects on the ultimate "consumer" of the artist's work. Are we certain we want to forbid the "consumer" certain obscenities, as the Eighteenth Amendment forbade certain beverages? Ah, you say, but alcohol in moderation is not an evil; the better analogy would be drug addiction.

It may be better but it is not very good. It is a lot easier to predict the effect of heroin on any normal body than to predict the effect of pornographic literature or art on any normal soul. To do the courts justice, this is one of the reasons they are having a difficult time with the obscenity issue. And it is by no means certain that the commission of "qualified persons," of which some reformers dream, would have a conspicuously easier time. Reactions to the "incent" are highly subjective. One of the few things we know about the matter is that to "the pure" almost everything is rotten!

But let us accept the analogy of drug addiction. Is it wiser to forbid the sale of heroin to addicts or to follow the British practice and license the addict? I take it the addict needs help and guidance, not only to release him from bondage to his drug but also to release him from whatever drove him to drugs in the first place. The mature man or woman with an addiction to pornographic photographs or to strip-tease may present us with the same temptation as the heroin addict: to treat the symptom under the illusion that we are treating the disease.

It is now high time that we raised the very practical question, What about children? I find in practice that even the most determined libertarian does not believe children present the same problem as adults. But I also find that the more enthusiastic would-be censors seize on these poor children as a reason for censoring everybody. In fact, these reformers remind one of our big business corporations, positively weeping over the damage that corporation taxes do to countless widows and orphans who live in penury on stock dividends. I should like in all seriousness to propose that we focus our ingenuity on protecting minors from things their parents cannot physically defend them from in our kind of industrial society, but that we refuse to reduce the intellectual and aesthetic diet of our adults to the ration suitable for a girls' boarding school. Otherwise stated, our rulers—the electorate—had best be protected from either the doctrines or the images that some censor, or indeed any censor, might deem injurious to them.

For the immature non-rulers, the case is different: all of Plato's concern for them is relevant. If you object that many of our voters are children in all respects but the number of years they have existed physically, I can only suggest that your objection comes too late. The crucial step was taken when they were given political responsibility. If, on the other hand, you object that as a practical matter, no community will tolerate obscenity, quite aside from the children, I shall first challenge the facts by pointing out that some communities tolerate enormously more "immorality" than those which operate in the Anglo-Saxon puritan tradition. Secondly, I shall urge that although Dr. Gallup is not alone in enjoying the art of estimating what our neighbors will tolerate, there is nevertheless for a free society a prior problem, and that is, what ought we to tolerate. The present essay is not an effort to guess how confused we are on the question of censorship; it is an effort to discover a principle for judging censorship. Any principle, no matter how wise, that we might discover will offer its peculiar difficulties of application.

I have said that our censors show signs of using children as a camel's nose to pry up our First-Amendment tent. Our censors also display an ingenuous inability to distinguish between what is evil and a necessary object of law, and what is evil but not a good object of law. But, surely, there are other ways of meeting evil than with police force, and it is sad that organized groups of Christians seem to prefer force. Too often their first step is to declare something "against the moral law" and their second to conclude that therefore we should call the police. Are not some of our church organizations really too lazy to teach morals and therefore hopeful that the police can frighten people or force people into being moral anyhow? And is it not perhaps this quickness to substitute force for dialectic that makes many liberals profoundly suspicious of the churches' political interventions? Some of my religious friends are fond of charging civil libertarians with a fuzzy, romantic, doctrinaire, and essentially empty view of law and freedom, and of being too lazy to think through the problem. Alas, they themselves exemplify regrettably one of the lazy man's chief weaknesses: his love of force.

I would therefore urge again that the only limits on "the preaching of false doctrines" are those, like parliamentary procedure, which promote the dialectic of those who govern the community, and not those that shut out certain views because they would be dangerous; and, secondly, that while minors should be protected from "indecent" books, plays, or films, this is no excuse for "protecting" grown men and women. More precisely, obscenity and impropriety in the arts, so far as the mature, voting public is concerned, should be met with competent criticism, not with policemen.

It is, of course, easier to call the police than to furnish competent criticism. It is also easier to close out a movie film than to devise means to restrict its showing to adults. We spend enormous time, money, and energy protecting "public morals." If we spent half as much protecting minors, who are still in the formative stage, and the other half on educating them to genuine adulthood, we should have no time left over in which to interfere with grown persons. We could then leave their problem to criticism, the quality of which could be expected to improve if it faced a new responsibility.

PART V: *Religion and the Free Society*

1

THE PRESENT EMBARRASSMENT
OF THE CHURCH

Gustave Weigel

I

Religion can contribute to the welfare of the general community; it can help society. My only worry is whether it should.

It certainly cannot be the prime purpose of religion to make secular society more beneficent and the secular enterprise more satisfactory. That can indeed be the consequent of religion. But consequents are not the goals of deliberation; they are casual accretions to the proper goals of a planned effort.

Perhaps it would not be taken amiss if we were to say that man is not for society, but that society is for man. Given the needs of the human being, society is necessary for their satisfaction. This does not mean that society exists to grant man the objects of his every caprice and uncriticized impulses. Society is a reality no less than the individual, and if the individual needs society, he must respect its being. The needs of man show that he is more than an atomic individual; he is also of necessity a member of society, which is posited by the very fact that man exists. In consequences, man must adjust to the collectivity. It is not the function of society to adjust to the isolated individual. But society must be human just as the individual is human.

Here is the nub of our problem. Neither the individual man nor secular society is an absolute. They are relative to each other. Just as we cannot expect society to accept every demand of the individual, so we cannot expect the individual to submit to whatsoever is commanded by society. The individual has rights which society cannot nullify and the commonwealth has rights which it cannot abdicate.

All historical malaise comes from the failure either of the individual to respect the rights of the collectivity or of the collectivity's tyrannical suppression of the rights of the individual. In our day we see it so concretely in the cold war which vexes the hearts of all the men of the world. Soviet Russia stands for community over the individual; the free society as championed by the United States stands for the individual over society. Both communities would anxiously object to this generalization. The Russians will insist that they are very much concerned with the individual and the Americans feel certain that they are preoccupied with the commonwealth. Both could bring much evidence to support their claims, and the evidence is convincing enough. Yet the original statement of the problem is valid, valid as a draftsman's linear drawing represents the solid object he is depicting.

In the wisdom man has achieved during the thousands of years he has lived on this little globe, conflicts, actual or possible, are settled by an appeal to a judge who is not identified with either of the conflicting parties. Here we have the solution of the social problem. We need an arbiter who will justly decide the rights of society and justly decide the rights of the individual. This judge can be neither society nor the individual.

But where can we find such a judge? That has always been the human problem. When the conflict is between the individual and society, society has in its favor the power of coercion and the individual has in his support the power of rebellion. The same situation exists when two communities are in conflict. In consequence the question of rights has usually been resolved by power.

Is the power of rebellion greater than the power of coercion? That is concretely the question which faces every generation in history. We are in a revolutionary moment. The rising of the East against the colonizing power of the western commonwealths shows very clearly that the power of rebellion is as great, if not greater than the power of coercion at the disposal of the western nations.

Now there is something irrational in this way of deciding rights. Power and right are on different planes of reality. Right can well be powerless and power can well be unrighteous. Neither can establish the other. The power of rebellion can counterbalance the power of coercion, but this leaves the whole question of right untouched.

These observations are by no means new. They have been recognized in every era of history. It is not surprising, then, to find that the sages of mankind have looked for something better and more rational to control the individual and society. It is amusing to find angry voices rail against the notion of original sin. Yet there is nothing more evident than original sin in the story of mankind. Man's impulse to the irrational is patent on every page of history, and the religious name for this impulse is original sin. The problem of human history is how to control original sin.

The older societies thought that they had a solution for the conflict of the individual with society. They put both the individual and society under God. God gave rights to each and God decided their disputes. God's action came through revelation and prophets made God's mind known. The prophet first manifested *torah*, the law. Then the prophet spoke the judgment of God on those who violated *torah*. In a God-fearing people this process was most effective. King and people knew they were under God, and they accepted His word as decisive.

But faith is a precarious thing. It can be lost, and when it goes, it is no longer possible to appeal to a revealing God. In this situation the wise men gave mankind another tribunal for the adjudication of conflict. Reason was impartial and uncommitted. Hence reason could control the affairs of man and society. If God is no longer present, then we turn to Natural Law, which is another way of speaking of the omnicompetence of reason.

However, the men who had rejected God saw that Reason with a capital R was another spelling for God, and out went the Natural Law as arbiter. If reason was written with a small r, then the question was: whose reason shall we follow?

That is where we are now and that is where we have been for many years. During this time of impasse, some optimistic voices simply proclaimed that the concrete conflict would be solved by power, for this is a beneficent drive in history which would insure that power in the long run would produce to the good for all, even though power is indifferent to right and wrong. There was no need to criticize power and bring it to judgment. Power is good, not perhaps in this or that case, but in the totality of its action. There was no reason over it and it was under no God. Hence reason and God were irrelevant factors in the discussion. Hence law itself was only the will of power, the will of the 51 percent. These had the power of coercion and that settled the matter.

In the century-old predicament we have reached a moment of disillusion. We can no longer accept this complacent submission to power. Power today is obviously fraught with the threat of destroying man, physically, culturally or both. It has to be judged and it has to be used in the light of judgment. Yet we are not prepared to recognize reason as an instrument of discovery. We still think it is only a device to implement the imperatives of arbitrary will. Hence there is no return to a belief in Natural Law, even though we hear isolated voices gingerly advocating it.

It is not surprising that in this situation the secular community is turning to the communities of faith to tame the monster of power roaring at the gates. The question we must ask however is whether in doing so the secular collectivity is not clutching at straws.

The secular community certainly does not want to be converted into a religious community. The insistence that civic society prescinds from religious commitment was never more visible than today. The political society feels quite magnanimous because it generously gives every citizen the right to be as religious or irreligious as he wishes. What then does the collectivity ask of its religious members? A favor in return for the favor of toleration granted. It is recognized that religion refuses to be intimidated by power. It has always stood up against it. The civic community is now asking that the men and women of religion harness this resistance to the chariot of the natural commonwealth. Religion, which before was tolerantly given the right to exist, is now invited to become an active dynamism in the common enterprise. Religion is now seen not merely as something to be tolerated but even as something to be used, and valuable because it can be used.

This innocent kindness of the natural civic society should not be a trap for religion. It easily can be. It is intoxicating to feel one's self esteemed after a long period of contempt. Good will and a spirit to please can stir the recipient of this new esteem. But the desire to please may be a subtle trend toward suicide. It is enlightening here to see what the Soviet government did during the last war. Every method to stimulate the defense of the land was used. As a result, the weakly masked persecution of religion was suspended. If the notion of Holy Russia helped Russians to fight the invader, then the notion of Holy Russia was encouraged. The priests who only a few years before were hampered and harassed, now received decorations for their defense of the fatherland. The government became kindly to religion. But there was no conversion, only accommodation.

Far be it from me to insinuate that the ideal relation of religion to secular society should be one of hostility. Reason itself suggests that there should be concord between a religious fellowship and the natural community in which it exists. Both collectivities should serve each other, though neither should be subservient to the other. However, what should be stressed is that religion deals with what concerns man ultimately, and therefore the ultimate allegiance must be religious. It may be a very bad religion, dedicated to an idol rather than to God, but it is a religion nonetheless. Any religion which does not divinize secular society will have an ultimate allegiance higher than its loyalty to the nation. Ancient Israel was a theocracy, but it did not adore the nation. Ancient Rome was not a theocracy but it did adore the state. In a free society, at least in principle, there is no preoccupation with what the people adore.

What then can a religion which does not adore the nation-state do for the civic community? It seems to me that it can fulfill its highest possibilities simply being true to itself. It must seek first the kingdom of God and its justice and all lesser goods will come as well. If there be any degree of validity in the religion, it will make for virtue. The more valid the religion the richer will be its manifestation of the virtues of unselfishness, sobriety, fulfillment of duty. These things are not just religious virtues but also positive contributions to the natural commonwealth, for the commonwealth cannot survive without them. It is precisely in this area that the civic community expects help from religion. The fruits of high religion are the love of man which results in help of the neighbor, self-control, industriousness, solidarity, patience and steadfastness. These fruits the political society wants. It does not care what they spring from. Often enough statesmen seem to think that religion has some kind of trick whereby these qualities can be produced, and they ask the churches for the trade-secret. One thinks of Simon Magus who when he saw the wonders caused by the imposition of hands by the apostles Peter and John, tried to buy the power. The trouble was that it was not for sale and no money could buy it. There was a power in Peter and John which they did not possess but which possessed them.

The higher religions are not merely seminaries of virtue. The virtue itself comes from a faith and the faith is the human reaction to divine revelation. According to St. Paul, faith comes from hearing. The revelation must be communicated to men, and those who communicate participate in the prophetic mission. The prophet speaks in the name of God. To this message faith can be given. We expect, then, that a valid religion will be prophetic. It will give witness to the divine message to which it clings in faith. In the secular community this witness is given. Faith is not a talent to be buried in the ground. Divine revelation is orientation and healing for those who believe, and the community which takes God at His word will be a sound society. As I understand Christian revelation, no natural community will ever surrender itself to God in faith. To believe, an inner grace is given, and grace is given to the elect. This is a hard doctrine, but it seems to be confirmed by the history of the world ever since the coming of revelation.

Even in the hypothesis that not all will believe, it yet remains true that the believer in love and enthusiasm will give witness to the faith that is in him. He will inevitably speak the good news to all his fellows to whom he is attracted in love by the very faith he possesses. Whether the neighbor accepts the witness does not particularly concern the prophet. He must speak even though no one will listen.

This prophetic function of religion is embarrassing to the secular community. It is disturbing; it is a source of division; it is a distraction from the concentration on the purely secular. Here is the paradox of the demand society makes. It wants the fruits of faith, but it does not want the prophetic root of those fruits. The prophet not only shows the way to salvation; he also utters judgment on the action of the world. This is resented by the unbeliever and the resentment can become bitter and cruel. According to the accounts of history the fate of the prophets was an unenviable one.

If a man is truly religious, he must be ready and resigned to hostility from the unbelievers. But he must not foment such hostility. The word of God is never repellent even when it condemns. It calls not to anger but to repentance. But given the selfishness of men, the prophet must not be surprised when instead of receiving a welcome, he receives abuse. Still he must give witness. He is a prophet by the mere fact that he has active faith.

Here we have the temptation which faces religion in our time. As I have already stated, religion serves the secular commonwealth by just being itself. It does not have to run the government; it cannot be one of the enlisted forces of defense. It lives in secular society but its life has a source and direction not to be derived from or even restricted by the commonwealth.

Secular society today is trying to make a deal with the churches. It is saying: Give us your unswerving support in the pursuit of the objectives we have before us; in return we will cover you with honor. This does not sound like the tempter's words when he showed Christ all the glories of the world and offered them to Him in return for adoration. Yet it may be the same thing.

I know that secularists will be irritated by such an observation. They are making their offer in all good faith and as far as they are aware, there is nothing diabolical about it. They point out that their objectives are noble ones, not unworthy of religion. They may well be right, but there is nevertheless a temptation at hand. The churches are being asked for unswerving loyalty and enthusiastic allegiance. Yet the church can give such allegiance only conditionally, never absolutely. If society is pursuing a virtuous goal, the church will spontaneously pursue the same goal. If society pursues a sinful objective, the church must refuse cooperation. And it will be the church which will make the decision as to the goodness of the goal. The church which must first seek the kingdom of God and its justice, cannot do otherwise and remain the church. This is the high command, the categorical imperative.

II

So far our meditation might suggest to the unwary that the church must remain coldly aloof from the interests of the secular community. Actually this has not been the burden of my thought. The only thesis so far proposed is that it is not the purpose of the church to save the republic nor is it the function of the church to be a ministry of defense for government. As was said twice before, the church will aid the secular community by just being itself. It makes little difference if the church be numerous or meager. In either case it will be a light on the mountain and a leaven in the mass.

Hence the only complaint the political society can make is that the church is not herself in a given time and place. Actually something of this kind appeared recently in an article in *The Nation*. I refer to C. Wright Mills' "A Pagan Sermon to the Christian Clergy." [1] I believe that Mr. Mills does not quite understand the nature of Christianity, but in his favor I must say that the line of thought he followed was that churches were not doing what was proper for them to do according to their own structures. He was not asking the churches to become instruments of the state; he bitterly

[1] Volume 186, No. 10, March 8, 1958; pp. 199-202.

complained that they did not do what by their own profession and tradition they should be doing. Concretely he found that the churches were not making their members aware of the monstrous immorality involved in modern public policy which relies at least in part on the threat that one nation can direct against another through atomic power. Mills believes that the churches are slavishly accommodating their message to the accepted prejudices of our environment. They are not trying to lead; they only follow.

In a sense I do not think that it is the role of the church to lead secular society. The church is here to give effective witness to the will of God. If anyone follows this message, it will be God's doing. If no one follows, it does not mean that the church failed in its mission. I think that Mills' latent error is that he supposes that the church should strive to be a secular good. This is never the church's obligation.

However, there is a valid ground in the exasperated criticism Mills made. An accommodating church is not being herself. Prophetic protest is an essential element of the church's preaching, and this protest must not be launched only against the little foibles of the individual but likewise against the gigantic immorality of public policy.

When the church is truly herself, the gospel will be preached and Christian action stimulated and organized in such a way as to be relevant to modern man. Old institutions can easily become bogged down by ancient habits originally formed to meet passing problems. The church is timeless; for that very reason she must be timely. No past moment is privileged that only in its terms can the gospel be heralded. The concerns of contemporary man must be the medium which the church uses to express the divine revelation. Antiquarianism has its charms but it is not to be a hobble on the divine word. If we cannot tolerate the notion of secular society making demands on the church, even less can we tolerate the notion of the church cutting herself off from the stream of human life in which she must perform her task.

Hence we do need religious activity in the problematic of our time. Religious thinkers in the light of revelation should give answers to the questions raised in our moment of history; they may not excuse themselves on the pretext that these questions are secular. The questions demand a religious answer, and that answer will be witness. Nor is it enough that the church deal with the issues in the genteel atmosphere of an ivory tower. The witness must come out into the street. Thought and action should be related. Action with no root in thought is sheer turmoil. Thought with no overflow into action is an esthetic narcosis. We need not only St. Thomas Aquinas making his glorious distinctions but also St. Francis wandering down the country roads singing the love of God and man for the refreshment of those who hear him. We need not only those who retire into caves on the mountain but also those who embroil themselves in crusades.

The church must make some kind of accommodation to the world. It is the accommodation of relevance. The church is in the world and nowhere else. There she lives and there she must work. The task of accommodation is always a hazardous job. Human beings can accommodate so much that they will cease to be what they were and become something thoroughly different. In her effort to accommodate, the church may become a mirror of the secular society to which it must prophesy. The faith of the church teaches her that God Himself will not allow her to undergo this total sea-change; rather He will save her but for this end He usually uses chastisement.

Whether the church is to undergo chastisement or not we cannot say. Yet her task is clear enough. Instead of telling secular society what it must do to save itself, it might be better for men of the church to tell the children of the church what they must do to live. It may well be the most effective contribution which the church can make to free society.

Perhaps three things stand out for religious men to do. Material abundance offers a great opportunity for ease, luxury and decadence. In such a situation virtue is weakened and materialism tends to stifle faith. In such a moment, and in this land the moment is now, austerity must be preached.

Nor is it enough to preach austerity by word alone. St. Francis not only preached poverty, he lived it as well. In order to be truly themselves the churches must voluntarily follow the example of ancient Nineveh excited by the threats of Jonah. Religious reform movements always included a return to simplicity of life where industriousness was the rule of being and sobriety the mark of faith. A consequent of such action is a morally stronger community made leaner by its fasting and more efficient in its effort to be creative under the command of God. Duty stands out more clearly than pleasure and when it does, the community can do almost anything. The call to austerity falls on deaf ears if it be directed to the secular community at large. The church must direct the cry to her own, and she can give motives higher than the well-being of the commonwealth. Here the church must act as church and in being the church she will aid the republic.

The second need of the church in our time is the deeper awareness of the reality of God in whom we live and move and have our being. In the hustle and bustle of today, it is hard for a man to think. We are rushing about in all directions with little attention to why we are moving at all. The world is becoming so visible that the invisible God is more hidden than ever. The man of faith today is a man of little faith. He seems to need prayer less because social organization gives him all he needs. But a self-sufficient humanity is man inflated with hybris, and hybris is the sin which the deity cannot tolerate in man.

Again it is not a question of speaking to the natural community, for in speaking to it, you must use the very media which bring about the sense of self-sufficiency. The church must speak to her own and get them to look away from the world with all its glamor and fascination, and turn to God. The church must preach retreat, though it need not be the retreat to the desert. It need only be a retreat to the heart where man can find the *Seelenfunklein* where God dwells. In God's presence man sees his own size and the presence of God gives man power to do and to suffer as he cannot do and suffer without God in view. The churches must preach prayer, must turn the mind of men to God. This will not take men out of the world, but it will show men God in the world, and they will act to please Him. It is well and good that we have monks and contemplatives, but something of the work they are engaged in must be shared by those who are not in monasteries and retreats.

The third thing we need is a truer and more effective love for all men, including those who are our enemies. Do good to them that hate you, is a religious message. Only through the force of faith is it possible. It is hardly necessary here to be dithyrambic about the beauties of love of one for the other. That song has been often sung. Yet the exhileration given to life by a brother aiding brother, by a consoler sharing the pain and suffering of his neighbor, needs to be pointed out. This is what the church must do in a society where welfare is a secular project, achieved by machine-like organizations moving on the plane of science rather than love. The church must bring out the ancient truth that every man is his brother's keeper and that it is not enough to refer him to a social agency.

Much of the good done in our society is done without love. Charity today means just the opposite of the word we use to cover the activity inspired by love. It often means condescending and heartless giving in order to be free of the sight of misery. Aid given in that spirit produces hatred, for the recipient is not so much helped as humiliated. Once more it is useless to speak to the civil society about the matter. It has its charity-machines which in machine-like fashion turn out their alms and assistance. There is little else that secular society can do, and it is wonderful that it does as much as it does. But men and women of faith who know that God is in all men and that God is loving and to be loved, will go to their neighbor in an entirely different spirit than the organizations of public welfare. It is the church working on those within the church which can effectively produce genuine charity.

III

Perhaps my remarks have not been practical from the viewpoint of the secularist. He will be disappointed when he hears that the best contribution the church can make to the plight of free society is to preach austerity, God-awareness and love, to the members of the church. I am sorry if he is disappointed, but as I see it, the church can do nothing else. She cannot construct programs of atomic-power control. She cannot propose public policy which will bring peace. These things are the proper and exclusive function of the secular community. The church cannot take them over, nor is she equipped by her own nature to deal with problems which are purely secular.

Yet there is something very practical in these reflections. It is not the practicality of gadgets and devices. It is the practicality of the real. To act follows on being. If being is stressed and enhanced, action will be its spontaneous offshoot. We must keep the concept of being foremost in our attention. We have been too much afflicted by worrying exclusively about action. The "practical" is often highly impractical.

The whole burden of my effusion has been that the church can help the free society only in one way. She helps by being herself genuinely and integrally. She cannot be state counselor, guide or governmental ministry. But if the church is herself, then the secular society will be aided.

Pointing this general truth to the problems of the moment in which we live, I have suggested that the church stress in its members three virtues which are proper to faith: austerity, God-consciousness and brotherly love. If the church does this, she is what she should be. The overflow of these virtues will strengthen, vivify and aid the free society.

I am dubious about other programs like those which would harness the churches to the effort of society. They seem to be based on a misunderstanding and degeneration of religion and in spite of their seeming high practicality are most impractical. They will neither help the church nor help our free society.

2

THE RELIGIOUS MESSAGE

Abraham Joshua Heschel

I

Little does religion ask of contemporary man. It is ready to offer comfort; it has no courage to challenge. It is ready to offer edification; it has no courage to break the idols, to shatter the callousness. The trouble is that religion has become "religion"—institution, dogma, securities. It is not an event anymore. Its acceptance involves neither risk nor strain. Religion has achieved respectability by the grace of society, and its representatives publish as a frontispiece the *nihil obstat* signed by social scientists.

There is no substitute for faith, no alternative for revelation, no surrogate for commitment. This we must remember in order to save our thought from confusion. And confusion is not a rare disease. We are guilty of committing the fallacy of misplacement. We define self-reliance and call it faith, shrewdness and call it wisdom, anthropology and call it ethics, literature and call it Bible, inner security and call it religion, conscience and call it God. However, nothing counterfeit can endure forever.

It is customary to blame secular science and anti-religious philosophy for the eclipse of religion in modern society. It would be more honest to blame religion for its own defeats. Religion declined not because it was refuted, but because it became irrelevant, dull, oppressive, insipid. When faith is completely replaced by creed, worship by discipline, love by habit; when the crisis of today is ignored because of the splendor of the past; when faith becomes an heirloom rather than a living fountain; when religion speaks only in the name of authority rather than with the voice of compassion, its message becomes meaningless.

Religion is an answer to ultimate questions. The moment we become oblivious to ultimate questions, religion becomes irrelevant, and its crisis sets in. The primary task of religious thinking is to rediscover the questions to which religion is an answer, to develop a degree of sensitivity to the ultimate questions which its ideas and acts are trying to answer.

Religious thinking is an intellectual endeavor out of the depths of reason. It is a source of cognitive insight into the ultimate issues of human existence. Religion is more than a mood or a feeling. Judaism, for example, is a way of thinking, not only a way of living. Unless we understand its categories, its mode of apprehension and evaluation, its teachings remain unintelligible.

It is not enough to call for good will. We are in desperate need of good thinking.

Our theme is religion and its relation to the free society. Such a relation can only be established if we suceed in rediscovering the intellectual relevance of the Bible.[1]

Now the most serious obstacle which modern men encounter in entering a discussion about the ideas of the Bible, is the absence of the problem to which the Bible refers. This, indeed, is the status of the Bible in modern society: it is a sublime answer, but we no longer know the question to which it responds. Unless we recover the question, there is no hope of understanding the Bible.

The Bible is an answer to the question, What does God require of Man? But to modern man, this question is suppressed by another one, namely, What does man demand of God? Modern man continues to ponder: What will I get out of life? What escapes his attention is the fundamental, yet forgotten question: What will life get out of me?

The alarming fact is that man is becoming "a fighter for needs" rather than "a fighter for ends," as defined by William James.

Absorbed in the struggle for the emancipation of the individual we have concentrated our attention upon the idea of human rights and overlooked the importance of human obligations. More

[1] *The Intellectual Relevance of the Bible,* the book which the author of this essay hopes to write.

and more the sense of commitment, which is so essential a component of human existence, was lost in the melting pot of conceit and sophistication. Oblivious to the fact of his receiving infinitely more than he is able to return, man began to consider his self as the only end. Caring only for his needs rather than for his being needed, he is hardly able to realize that rights are anything more than legalized interests.

Needs are looked upon today as if they were holy, as if they contained the totality of existence. Needs are our gods, and we toil and spare no effort to gratify them. Suppression of a desire is considered a sacrilege that must inevitably avenge itself in the form of some mental disorder. We worship not one but a whole pantheon of needs and have come to look upon moral and spiritual norms as nothing but personal desires in disguise.

Specifically, need denotes the absence or shortage of something indispensable to the well-being of a person, evoking the urgent desire for satisfaction. The term "need" is generally used in two ways: one denoting the actual lack, an objective condition, and the other denoting the awareness of such a lack. It is in the second sense, in which need is synonymous with interest, namely "an unsatisfied capacity corresponding to an unrealized condition" that the term is used here.

Every human being is a cluster of needs, yet these needs are not the same in all men nor unalterable in any one man. There is a fixed minimum of needs for all men, but no fixed maximum for any man. Unlike animals, man is the playground for the unpredictable emergence and multiplication of needs and interests, some of which are indigenous to his nature, while others are induced by advertisement, fashion, envy, or come about as miscarriages of authentic needs. We usually fail to discern between authentic and artificial needs and, misjudging a whim for an aspiration, we are thrown into ugly tension. Most obsessions are the perpetuation of such misjudgments. In fact, more people die in the epidemics of needs than in the epidemics of disease. To stem the expansion of man's needs, which in turn is brought about by technological and social advancement, would mean to halt the stream on which civilization is riding. Yet the stream unchecked may sweep away civilization itself, since the pressure of needs turned into aggressive interests is the constant cause of wars and increases in direct proportion to technological progress.

We cannot make our judgments, decisions and directions for action dependent upon our needs. The fact is that man who has found out so much about so many things knows neither his own heart nor his own voice. Many of the interests and needs we cherish are imposed on us by the conventions of society; they are not indigenous to our essence. While some of them are necessities, others, as I said before, are fictitious, and adopted as a result of convention, advertisement or sheer envy.

The contemporary man believes he has found the philosopher's stone in the concept of needs. But who knows his true needs? How are we going to discern authentic from fictitious needs, necessities from make-believes?

Having absorbed an enormous amount of needs and having been taught to cherish the high values, such as justice, liberty, faith, as private or national interests, we are beginning to wonder whether needs and interests should be relied upon. While it is true that there are interests which all men have in common, most of our private and national interests, as asserted in daily living, divide and antagonize rather than unite us.

Interest is a subjective, dividing principle. It is the excitement of feeling, accompanying special attention paid to some object. But do we pay sufficient attention to the demands for universal justice? In fact, the interest in universal welfare is usually blocked by the interest in personal welfare, particularly when it is to be achieved at the price of renouncing one's vested interests. It is just because the power of interests is tyrannizing our lives, determining our views and actions, that we lose sight of the values that count most.

Short is the way from need to greed. Evil conditions make us seethe with evil needs, with mad dreams. Can we afford to pursue all our innate needs. even our will for power?

In the tragic confusion of interests, in which every one of us is caught, no distinction seems to be as indispensable as the distinction between right and wrong interests. Yet the concepts of right and wrong, to be standards in our dealing with interests, cannot themselves be interests. Determined as they are by temperament, bias, background and environment of every individual and group, needs are our problems rather than our norms. They are in need of, rather than the origins of, standards.

He who sets out to employ the realities of life as means for satisfying his own desires will soon forfeit his freedom and be degraded to a mere tool. Acquiring things, he becomes enslaved to them; in subduing others, he loses his own soul. It is as if unchecked covetousness were double-faced; a sneer and subtle vengeance behind a captivating smile. We can ill afford to set up needs, an unknown, variable, vacillating and eventually degrading factor, as a universal standard, as a supreme, abiding rule or pattern for living.

We feel jailed in the confinement of personal needs. The more we indulge in satisfactions, the deeper is our feeling of oppressiveness. To be an iconoclast of idolized needs, to defy our own immoral interests, though they seem to be vital and have long been cherished, we must be able to say *no* to ourselves in the name of a higher *yes*. Yet our minds are late, slow and erratic. What can give us the power to curb the deference to wrong needs, to detect spiritual fallacies, to ward off false ideals and to wrestle with inattentiveness to the unseemly and holy?

This, indeed, is the purpose of our religious traditions: to keep alive the higher "yes" as well as the power of man to say "Here I am"; to teach our minds to understand the true demand and to teach our conscience to be present. Too often, we misunderstand the demand; too often the call goes forth, and history records our conscience as absent.

Religion has adjusted itself to the modern temper by proclaiming that it too is the satisfaction of a need. This conception, which is surely diametrically opposed to the prophetic attitude, has richly contributed to the misunderstanding and sterilization of religious thinking. To define religion primarily as a quest for personal satisfaction, as the satisfaction of a human need, is to make of it a refined sort of magic. Did the thunderous voice at Sinai proclaim the ten Words in order to satisfy a need? The people felt a need for a graven image, but that need was condemned. The people were homesick for the fleshpots of Egypt. They asked: Give us flesh. And the Lord gave them spirit, not only flesh.

The Bible does not begin with man, or the history of religion, or man's need for God. "At the beginning God created heaven and earth." To begin with needs is a sign of man's pitiful perspective.

Religion is spiritual effrontery. Its root is in our bitter sense of inadequacy, in a thirst which can only be stilled by greater thirst, in the embarrassment that we really do not care for God, in the discovery that our religious need is utterly feeble, that we do not feel any need for God.

We must beware of converting needs into ends, interests into norms. The task is precisely the opposite: it is to convert ends into needs, to convert the divine commandment into a human concern.

Religion is not a way of satisfying needs. It is an answer to the question: Who needs man? It is an awareness of being needed, of man being a need of God. It is a way of sanctifying the satisfaction of authentic needs.

It is an inherent weakness of religion not to take offence at the segregation of God, to forget that the true sanctuary has no walls. Religion has often suffered from the tendency to become an end in itself, to seclude the holy, to become parochial, self-indulgent, self-seeking; as if the task were not to ennoble human nature but to enhance the power and beauty of its institutions or to enlarge the body of doctrines. It has often done more to canonize prejudices than to wrestle for truth; to petrify the sacred than to sanctify the secular. Yet the task of religion is to be a challenge to the stabilization of values.

II

The mind of the prophets was not religion-centered. They dwelt more on the affairs of the royal palace, on the ways and views of the courts of justice, than on the problems of the priestly rituals at the temple of Jerusalem.

We today are shocked when informed about *an increase* in juvenile delinquency, or *an increase* in the number of crimes committed in our city. The normal amount of juvenile delinquency, the normal number of crimes does not cause us to be dismayed. At this very moment somewhere throughout the nation crimes are being committed.

The sort of crimes, and even the amount of delinquency that fill the prophets of Israel with dismay do not go beyond that which we regard as normal, as a typical ingredient of social dynamics. A single act of injustice—to us it is slight, to the prophet it is a disaster.

Turning from the discourses of the great metaphysicians to the orations of the prophets, one may feel as if he were going down from the realm of the sublime to an area of trivialities. Instead of dealing with the timeless issues of being and becoming, of matter and form, of definitions and demonstrations, one is thrown into orations about widows and orphans, about the corruption of judges and affairs of the market place. The prophets make so much ado about paltry things, employing the most excessive language in speaking about flimsy subjects. So what if somewhere in ancient Palestine poor people have not been treated properly by the rich? So what if some old women found pleasure and edification in worshipping "the Queen of Heaven"? Why such immoderate excitement? Why such intense indignation?

Their breathless impatience with injustice may strike us as hysteria. We ourselves witness continually acts of injustice, manifestations of hypocrisy, falsehood, outrage, misery, but we rarely get indignant or overly excited. To the prophets a minor, commonplace sort of injustice assumes almost cosmic proportions.

> Be appalled, O heavens, at this,
> Be shocked, be utterly desolate, says the Lord.
> For My people have committed two evils:
> They have forsaken Me,
> The fountain of living waters
> And hewed out cisterns for themselves,
> Broken cisterns that hold no water.
>
> Jeremiah 2:12-13

They speak and act as if the sky were about to collapse because Israel had become unfaithful to God.

Is not the size of their indignation, is not the size of God's anger in disproportion to its cause? How should one explain such moral and religious excitability, such extreme impetuosity?

The prophet's words are outbursts of violent

emotions. His rebuke is harsh and relentless. But if such deep sensitivity to evil is to be called hysterical, what name should be given to the deep callousness to evil which the prophet bewails? "They drink from bowls of wine, and anoint themselves with the finest oils; but they are not pained by the crushing of Joseph" (Amos 6:6).

The niggardliness of our moral comprehension, the incapacity to sense the depth of misery caused by our own failures, is a fact which no subterfuge can elude. Our eyes are witness to the callousness and cruelty of man, but our heart tries to obliterate the memories, to calm the nerves, and to silence our conscience.

The prophet is a man who feels fiercely. God has thrust a burden upon his soul, and he is bowed and stunned at man's fierce greed. Frightful is the agony of man; no human voice can convey its full terror. Prophecy is the voice that God has lent to the silent agony, a voice to the plundered poor, to the profaned riches of the world. It is a form of living, a crossing point of God and man. God is raging in the prophets' words.

The prophets had disdain for those to whom God was comfort and security; to them God was a challenge, an incessant demand. He is compassion, but not a compromise; justice, but not inclemency. Tranquillity is unknown to the soul of a prophet. The miseries of the world give him no rest. While others are callous, and even callous to their callousness and unaware of their insensitivity, the prophets remain examples of supreme impatience with evil, distracted by neither might or applause, by neither success or beauty. Their intense sensitivity to right and wrong is due to their intense sensitivity to God's concern for right and wrong. They feel fiercely because they hear deeply.

The prophets tried to overcome the isolationism of religion. It is the prophets who teach us that the problem of living does not arise with the question of how to take care of the rascals, of how to prevent delinquency or hideous crimes. The problem of living begins with the realization of how we all blunder in dealing with our fellow men. The silent atrocities, the secret scandals, which no law can prevent, are the true seat of moral infection. The problem of living begins, in fact, in relation to our own selves, in the handling of our emotional functions, in the way we deal with envy, greed, and pride. What is first at stake in the life of man is not the fact of sin, of the wrong and corrupt, but the neutral acts, the needs. Our possessions pose no less a problem than our passions. The primary task, therefore, is not how to deal with the evil, but how to deal with the neutral, how to deal with needs.

The central commandment is in relation to the person. But religion today has lost sight of the person.

Religion has become an impersonal affair, an institutional loyalty. It survives on the level of activities rather than in the stillness of commitment. It has fallen victim to the belief that the real is only that which is capable of being registered by fact-finding surveys.

By religion is meant what is done publicly rather than that which comes about in privacy. The chief virtue is social affiliation rather than conviction.

Inwardness is ignored. The spirit has become a myth. Man treats himself as if he were created in the likeness of a machine rather than the likeness of God. The body is his god, and its needs are its prophets. Having lost his awareness of his sacred image, he became deaf to the command: to live in a way which is compatible with his image.

Religion without a soul is as viable as a man without a heart. Social dynamics is no substitute for meaning. Yet, the failure to realize the fallacy of such substitution seems to be common in our days.

Perhaps this is the most urgent task: to save the inner man from oblivion, to remind ourselves that we are a duality of mysterious grandeur and pompous dust. Our future depends upon our appreciation of the reality of the inner life, of the splendor of thought, of the dignity of wonder and reverence. This is the most important thought: God has a stake in the life of man, of every man. But this idea cannot be imposed from without; it must be discovered by every man; it cannot be preached, it must be experienced.

When the Voice of God spoke at Sinai, it did

not begin by saying, "I am the Lord your God Who created heaven and earth." It began by saying "I am the Lord your God who brought you out of the land of Egypt, out of the house of bondage." Judaism is not only deliverance from external slavery, but also freedom from false fears and false glories, from fashion, from intellectual will-o'-the-wisps. In our souls we are subject to causes; in our spirits we are free, beholding the uncompromising.

The most commanding idea that Judaism dares to think is that freedom, not necessity, is the source of all being. The universe was not caused, but created. Behind mind and matter, order and relations, the freedom of God obtains. The inevitable is not eternal. All compulsion is a result of choice. A tinge of that exemption from necessity is hiding in the folds of the human spirit.

We are not taught to feel accused, to bear a sense of boundless guilt. We are asked to feel elated, bred to meet the tasks that never end.

Every child is a prince; every man is obliged to feel that the world was created for his sake. Man is not the measure of all things, but the means by which to accomplish all tasks.

As a free being the Jew must accept an enormous responsibility. The first thing a Jew is told is: you can't let yourself go, get into harness, carry the yoke of the Kingdom of Heaven. He is told to bear loads of responsibility. He is told to abhor self-complacency, to enjoy freedom of choice. He has been given life and death, good and evil, and is urged to choose, to discriminate. Yet freedom is not only the ability to choose and to act, but also the ability to will, to love. The predominant feature of Jewish teaching throughout the ages is a sense of constant obligation.

We are taught to prefer truth to security, to maintain loyalty even at the price of being in the minority. It is inner freedom that gives man the strength to forego security, the courage to remain lonely in the multitude.

Judaism is forever engaged in a bitter battle against man's deeply rooted belief in fatalism and its ensuing inertia in social, moral and spiritual conditions. Abraham started in rebellion against his father and the gods of his time. His great distinction was, not in being loyal and conforming, but in defying and initiating. He was loved by the Lord not for ancestral worship but because he taught his descendants "to keep to the way of the lord, to do righteousness and justice" (Genesis 18:19).

III

We all share a supreme devotion to the hard won freedoms of the American people. Yet, to be worthy of retaining our freedoms we must not lose our understanding of the essential nature of freedom. Freedom means more than mere emancipation. It is primarily freedom of conscience, bound up with inner allegiance. The danger begins when freedom is thought to consist in the fact that "I can act as I desire." This definition not only overlooks the compulsions which often lie behind our desires; it reveals the tragic truth that freedom may develop within itself the seed of its own destruction. The will is not an ultimate and isolated entity, but determined by motives beyond its own control. *To be* what one wants to be, is also not freedom, since the wishes of the ego are largely determined by external factors.

Freedom is not a principle of uncertainty, the ability to act without a motive. Such action would be chaotic and sub-rational, rather than free.

Although political and social freedom must include all this, even the freedom to err—its true essence is in man's ability to surpass himself, even to act against his inclinations and in defiance of his own needs and desires, to sacrifice prejudice even if it *hurts*, to give up superstition even when it claims to be a doctrine.

Freedom is the liberation from the tyranny of the self-centered ego. It comes about in moments of transcending the self as an act of spiritual ecstasy, of stepping out of the confining framework of routine reflexive concern. Freedom presupposes *the capacity for sacrifice.*

Although all men are potentially free, it is our sacred duty to safeguard all those political, social, and intellectual conditions which will enable every man to bring about the concrete actualization of freedom which is the essential prerequisite of creative achievement.

The shock of radical amazement, the humility born in awe and reverence, the austere discipline of unremitting inquiry and self-criticism are acts of liberating man from the routine way of looking only at those features of experience which are similar and regular and open his soul to the unique and transcendent. This sensitivity to the novel and unprecedented is the foundation of God-awareness and of the awareness of the preciousness of all beings. It leads from reflexive concern and the moral and spiritual isolation which is the result of egocentricity to a mode of responding to each new and unique experience in terms of broader considerations, wider interests, deeper appreciation and new, as yet unrealized values.

As the object of divine transitive concern man is; knowing himself to be the object of divine concern and responding through acts of his own transitive concern *he is free.*

The meaning of freedom is not exhausted by deliberation, decision, and responsibility, although it must include all this. The meaning of freedom presupposes an openness to transcendence, and man has to be *responsive* before he can become *responsible.*

Man's true fulfillment cannot be reached by the isolated individual, and his true good depends on communion with, and participation in, that which transcends him. Each challenge from beyond the person is unique, and each response must be new and creative. Freedom is an act of engagement of the self to the spirit, a spiritual event.

Loyalty to freedom means loyalty to the substance of freedom. But such loyalty must be actualized again and again. Here our way of living must change: it must open the sight of sublime horizons under which we live.

Refusal to delegate the power to make ultimate decisions to any human institution, derives its strength either from the awareness of one's mysterious dignity or from the awareness of one's ultimate responsibility. But that strength breaks down in the discovery that one is unable to make a significant choice. Progressive vulgarization of society may deprive man of his ability to appreciate the sublime burden of freedom. Like Esau he may be ready to sell his birth-right for a pot of lentils.

A major root of freedom lies in the belief that man, every man, is too good to be the slave of another man. However, the dynamics of our society, the cheapening and trivialization of existence, continues to corrode that belief. The uniqueness and sacred preciousness of man is being refuted with an almost cruel consistency. I do not mean the anthropological problem whether we are descendants of the monkeys. What I have in mind is the fact that we are being treated as if there were little difference between man and monkey. Much that is being done, e.g. in the name of entertainment is an insult to the soul. What is involved is not demoralization; much of it may be morally neutral. What is involved is dehumanization; so much of it is a continual process of intellectual deprivation. Sensitivity to words is one of the many casualties in that process.

Words have become pretexts in the technique of evading the necessity of honest and genuine expression. Sometimes it seems as if we were all engaged in the process of liquidating the English language. But words are the vessels of the spirit. And when the vessels are broken, our relationship to the spirit becomes precarious.

To be free one must attain a degree of independence. Yet, the complexities of society have enmeshed contemporary man in a web of relationships which make his independence most precarious.

Inherent in man is the desire to be in agreement with others. Yet, today with a mass of miscellaneous associations and unprecedented excitements, it is a grim task, indeed, to agree with all and to retain the balance of integrity.

Loaded with more vulnerable interests than he is able to protect, bursting with fears of being squeezed by a multiplicity of tasks and responsibilities, modern man feels too insecure to remain upright.

Good and evil have always had a tendency to live in promiscuity, but in more integrated societies man, it seems, found it easier to discriminate between the two, while in our turbulent times circumstances often stupefy our power of discernment; it is as if many of us have become value-blind in the epidemics of needs.

The glory of a free society lies not only in the consciousness of my right to be free, and my capacity to be free, but also in the realization of my fellow-man's right to be free, and his capacity to be free. The issue we face is how to save man's belief in his capacity to be free. Our age may be characterized as the *age of suspicion*. It has become an axiom that the shortest way to the understanding of man is to suspect his motives. This seems to be the contemporary version of the Golden Rule: *Suspect thy neighbor as thyself*. Suspicion breeds suspicion. It creates a chain-reaction. Honesty is not necessarily an anachronism.

The insecurity of freedom is a bitter fact of historic experience. In times of unemployment, vociferous demagogues are capable of leading the people into a state of mind in which they are ready to barter their freedom for any bargain. In times of prosperity hidden persuaders are capable of leading the same people into selling their conscience for success. Unless a person learns how to rise daily to a higher plane of living, to care for that which surpasses his immediate needs, will he in a moment of crisis insist upon loyalty to freedom?

The threat to freedom lies in the process of reducing human relations to a matter of fact. Human life is not a drama anymore, it is a routine. Uniqueness is suppressed, repetitiveness prevails. We teach our students how to recognize the labels, not how to develop a taste. Standardization corrodes the sense of ultimate significance. Man to his own self becomes increasingly vapid, cheap, insignificant. Yet without the sense of ultimate significance and ultimate preciousness of my own existence, freedom becomes a hollow phrase.

The central problem of this generation is emptiness in the heart, the decreased sensitivity to the imponderable quality of the spirit, the collapse of communication between the realm of tradition and the inner world of the individual. The central problem is that we do not know how to think, how to pray, or how to cry, or how to resist the deceptions of the silent persuaders. There is no community of those who worry about integrity.

One of the chief problems of contemporary man is the problem: what to do with time? Most of our life we spend time in order to gain space, namely things of space. Yet when the situation arrives in which no things of space may be gained, the average man is at a loss as to what to do with time.

With the development of automation the number of hours to be spent professionally will be considerably reduced. The four day week may become a reality within this generation. The problem will arise: What to do with so much leisure time? The problem will be *too much* time rather than too little time. But too much time is a breeding ground for crime. Idleness is unbearable, and the most popular method to solve the problem of time is to kill time. Yet time is life, and to kill time is murder.

The average man has not only forgotten how to be alone; he finds it even difficult to be with his fellow man. He not only runs away from himself; he runs away from his family. To children "Honor your father and your mother," is an irrational commandment. The normal relationship is dull; deviation is where pleasure is found.

The average man does not know how to stand still, how to appreciate a moment, an event for its own sake. When witnessing an important event or confronted with a beautiful sight, all he does is take a picture. Perhaps this is what our religious traditions must teach the contemporary man: to stand still and to behold, to stand still and to hear.

Judaism claims that the way to nobility of the soul is the art of sanctifying time. Moral dedications, acts of worship, intellectual pursuits are means in the art of sanctification of time. Personal concern for justice in the market place, for integrity in public affairs and in public relations are a prerequisite for our right to pray.

Acts of worship counteract the trivialization of existence. Both involve the person, and give him a sense of living in ultimate relationships. Both of them are ways of teaching man how to stand alone and not be alone, of teaching man that God is a refuge, not a security.

But worship comes out of wisdom, out of insight, it is not an act of insight. Learning, too, is a religious commandment. Learning is an indispensable form of purification as well as ennoblement. I do not mean memorization, erudition; I mean the very act of study, of being involved in wisdom, and of being overwhelmed by the marvel and mystery of God's creation.

Religion's major effort must be to counteract the deflation of man, the trivialization of human existence. Our religious traditions claim that man is capable of sacrifice, discipline, of moral and spiritual exaltation, that every man is capable of an ultimate commitment.

Ultimate commitment includes the consciousness of being accountable for the acts we perform under freedom; the awareness that what we own we owe; the capacity for repentance; that a life without the service of God is a secret scandal.

Faith in God cannot be forced upon man. The issue is not only lack of faith but the vulgarization of faith, the misunderstanding and abuse of freedom. Our effort must involve a total reorientation about the nature of man and the world. And our hope lies in the certainty that all men are capable of sensing the wonder and mystery of existence, that all men have a capacity for reverence. Awe, reverence precedes faith; it is at the root of faith. We must grow in awe in order to reach faith. We must be guided by awe to be worthy of faith. Awe is "the beginning and gateway of faith, the first precept of all, and upon it the whole world is established."

The grandeur and mystery of the world that surrounds us is not something which is perceptible only to the elect. All men are endowed with a sense of wonder, with a sense of mystery. But our system of education fails to develop it and the anti-intellectual climate of our civilization does much to suppress it. Mankind will not perish for lack of information; it may collapse for want of appreciation.

Education for reverence, the development of a sense of awe and mystery, is a prerequisite for the preservation of freedom.

We must learn how to bridle the outrageous presumption of modern man, to cultivate a sense of wonder and reverence, to develop an awareness that something is asked of man. Freedom is a burden that God has thrust upon man. Freedom is something we are responsible for. If we succeed, we will help in the redemption of the world; if we fail, we may be crushed by its abuse. Freedom as man's unlimited lordship is the climax of absurdity, and the central issue we face is man's false sense of sovereignty.

Tragic is the role of religion in contemporary society. The world is waiting to hear the Voice, and those who are called upon to utter the word are confused and weak in faith. "The voice of the Lord is powerful, the voice of the Lord is full of majesty" (Psalms 29:3). Where is its power? Where is its majesty?

A story is told about a community where a man was accused of having transgressed the seventh commandment. The leaders of the community went to the Rabbi and voicing their strong moral indignation demanded stern punishment of the sinner. Thereupon the Rabbi turned his face to the wall and said: "O, Lord, Thy glory is in heaven, Thy presence on earth is invisible, imperceptible. In contrast to Thy invisibility, the object of that man's passion stood before his eyes, full of beauty and enravishing his body and soul. How could I punish him?"

R. Simon said: "When the Holy One, blessed be He, came to create Adam, the ministering angels formed themselves into groups and parties, some of them saying, 'Let him be created,' whilst others urged, 'Let him not be created.' Thus it is written, Love and Truth fought together, Righteousness and Peace combatted each other (Psalms 85:11): Love said, 'Let him be created, because he will dispense acts of love'; Truth said, 'Let him not be created, because he is compounded of falsehood'; Righteousness said, 'Let him be created, because he will perform righteous deeds'; Peace said, 'Let him not be created because he is full of strife.' What did the Lord do? He took Truth and cast it to the ground. Said the ministering angels before the Holy One, blessed be He, 'Sovereign of the

Universe! Why dost Thou despise Thy seal? Let Truth arise from the earth!' Hence it is written, Let truth spring up from the earth (Psalms 85:12)."

God had to bury truth in order to create man.

How does one ever encounter the truth? The truth is underground, hidden from the eye. Its nature and man's condition are such that he can neither produce nor invent it. However, there is a way. If you bury the lies, truth will spring up. Upon the grave of the specious we encounter the valid. Much grave digging had to be done. The most fatal trap into which religious thinking may fall is *the equation of faith with expediency*. The genuine task of our traditions is to educate a sense for the inexpedient, a sensitivity to God's demand.

Perhaps we must begin by disclosing *the fallacy of absolute expediency*. God's voice may sound feeble to our conscience. Yet there is a divine cunning in history which seems to prove that the wages of absolute expediency is disaster. We must not tire of reminding the world that something is asked of man, of every man; that the value of charity is not to be measured in terms of public relations. Foreign aid when offered to underdeveloped countries, for the purpose of winning friends and influencing people, turns out to be a boomerang. Should we not learn how to detach expediency from charity? The great failure of American policy is not in public relations. The great failure is in private relations.

The spirit is a still small voice, and the masters of vulgarity use loud-speakers. The voice has been stifled, and many of us have lost faith in the possibility of a new perceptiveness.

Discredited is man's faith in his own integrity. We question man's power to sense any ultimate significance. We question the belief in the compatibility of existence with spirit.

Yet, man is bound to break the chains of despair, to stand up against those who deny him the right and the strength to believe wholeheartedly. Ultimate truth may be hidden from man, yet the power to discern between the valid and the specious has not been taken from us.

Surely God will always receive a surprise of a handful of fools—who do not fail. There will always remain a spiritual underground where a few brave minds continue to fight. Yet our concern is not how to worship in the catacombs but rather how to remain human in the skyscrapers.

3

FREEDOM AND THE ULTIMATE CONCERN

Paul Tillich

I

I feel a certain uneasiness in talking about Religion and the Free Society. What does the term "free society" mean? When one uses it, does one have in mind the catchword "the free world" (I think then of Spain, South America and Formosa); or does one mean the nations where a democratic constitution actually works, as in the Anglo-Saxon countries; or does one mean an ideal which will become a reality sometime in the future; or does one mean the Kingdom of God, which never will become a reality in time and space for the simple reason that man always has the freedom to surrender his freedom?

When I started preparing these remarks, I immediately excluded the last of these four meanings because in the free society which is the Kingdom of God, there will be no religion; as the Book of Revelation tells us, God will dwell amongst them and they will not have a temple. I excluded also the first meaning of the word because it is produced for propaganda purposes and is a very artificial concept. What remains then are the second and third, namely, the present democratic countries, and an ideal "free society" which can at least be imagined as a possible development within history.

This, I think, is the only way in which it is meaningful and realistic to discuss the question of Religion and the Free Society. So I repeat that under the concept of free society, I understand the actual democracies of the present day seen from the point of view of their highest possibilities in time and space. On this basis I asked myself what is the function of religion in developing and preserving such democracies and transforming them from their present reality to their ideal possibilities.

But even after I overcame my initial uneasiness about the title, "Religion and the Free Society," I met still another one: Can religion be used as a tool for something else? And the answer of course was no. If religion is the state of being ultimately concerned, then it cannot be the tool for something else. The ultimate cannot be the tool for something non-ultimate.

Even the free society or the ideal democracy is not ultimate. Religion is ultimate. The ideal democracy may disappear, and the meaning of life for those who are bound in a total tyranny is not necessarily lost. They can preserve their ultimate concern even in chains. We know about the Christian prisoners in the Roman copper mines. They had no free society, but they had something else, and this something else never can be made into a tool for even the best free society.

This limits the very large concept of the subject to perhaps one question: Are there consequences, detrimental or beneficial, which flow from the strong religious consciousness found in many people within the free society?

Now in my first consideration I want to ask the question whether religion may endanger a free society. I think there are forces in religion which always have and always will resist the development of a free society. Four of these forces can be named: a religious conservatism, a religious authoritarianism, a religious intolerance, and a religious transcendentalism. If we discuss seriously the problem of religion and a free society, we certainly cannot evade these issues; current history has made them powerfully visible and the memory of thousands of years of past history has impressed them on the unconscious of everybody living today. How can these forces in religion be overcome by religion itself?

The conservative character of religion is based, first, on the unconditional character of the religious concern; secondly, on the unapproachable nature of the unconditional, which remains a mystery even after it has been revealed; thirdly, on the fact that we have only the barest manifestations of the ultimate, of the holy, in time and space; and, finally, on our tendency to confuse the holy itself with those who bear it to us.

Here are five reasons why the conservatism found in every religion may endanger a free society. Of course, to adhere to the bearers of the holy has in itself the quality of holiness. Devotion to holy objects, be they persons, events, books or rituals may be a holy experience. That which is unconditional, meaningful and serious is embodied in them and cannot appear to us except by being embodied in them.

But it follows then that out of this, an institutional conservatism arises. The institutions, persons, books, rituals, objects are invested with a taboo. You may not touch them; if you do touch them, either in reality, physically, or in thought, critically, a feeling of guilt develops. There is always the feeling of guilt. I do not know anybody who has not experienced it.

Now, then, the question arises, Can a society be called free in which the freedom to criticize given forms and traditions means that a sacred taboo is broken? This is my first question.

The second involves the authoritarian character of religion. The main inhibition against any radical criticism of religious traditions is the authority which the religions give to their own past and those who represent it. Is a society free if it is subject, either partly or totally, to a religious authority which can at any moment interfere with the institutions of society and perhaps even with the free society itself; which, for instance, can organize masses of voters who because of this guilt feeling about taboos are unable to resist the commands they have received? This is particularly pointed when the ultimate source of such commands are foreign to the traditions out of which the free society itself was born.

The next point to consider is the intolerance of religion. What is tolerance? It can be many things. Is it lack of conviction? Is it indifference to a special problem? Is it charity? Or is it itself a religious conviction, and if so, how is tolerance possible if religion is a matter of ultimate concern?

We must first of all acknowledge that even in the greatest representatives of the idea of tolerance—I am thinking of John Locke's letters on the subject—there are limits of tolerance. Perhaps it is not very well known that Locke wanted to exclude two groups, the Catholics and the atheists. The unconditional truths of a religiously consecrated liberal society is Locke's absolute; on the basis of this absolute he is intolerant against those who are not liberal—he specifically mentioned Catholics—and those who deny religious consecration—he meant the atheists.

Again, I ask a question: Is a free society, which is certainly a society of tolerance, possible, or does it contradict human nature, if even the greatest prophets of tolerance limited their tolerance? Is absolute tolerance possible for any group which holds ultimate convictions?

The transcendent character of religion, the fourth point I want to mention, means that religion emphasizes the vertical line of other-worldliness and detours many people from the horizontal line of political concern. I think of the example offered by the Lutheran churches in Germany. They were indifferent to political events even after Hitler came to power and up to the moment when the political powers interfered with the Church; not a moment before did they offer a word of protest against the persecution of the Jews or the murders which had been committed by Hitler before he came to power.

The example of religious socialism in Germany is also interesting. I was myself a member of this movement in the Twenties. We were often accused of weakening the dynamic power of the socialist movement because we emphasized the spiritual concerns which were completely forgotten by the socialist parties and their leaders. It was hard for us to answer. If you don't believe that the classless society or the Kingdom of God on earth is just around the corner, is your dynamic power as great as those who do believe it? But if you believe it, you are in for a great metaphysical disappointment, for you expect something ultimate which is not ultimate.

II

Religion enables the growth and life of a free society in three ways: First, by judging itself within the free society; second, by forming the bearers of the free society; and third, by judging the life of the free society.

First, religion judging religion. This, of course, is the first and basic point. There are two elements in every religion, the unconditional and the concrete concern. When we say that religion is the ultimate or unconditional or infinite concern, we immediately show that religion has two elements; one element involves the experience of something unconditionally serious, or something which reaches into that which is ultimate; the second element is the concrete expression of this ultimate concern in the forms of some special tradition, with its own symbols, doctrines, rights and constitutions.

Now, the first element certainly does not endanger any society. It gives religion the power to judge itself. The liberal critics of religion forget one thing. They forget that the roots of criticism historically lie in the self-criticism of the original religions. Prophets and seers lash out against priests, and after they have changed the system created by the priests through their criticism, another priesthood is established. This is the dialectic of religious life everywhere. In each case, the confusion of the holy object with the holy itself, something finite's being turned into something infinite, is the point of the prophetic attack.

This relation of the finite to the infinite is what endangers the free society. The attack of the prophets is based on the principle of justice being applied against all "holy" injustices; it rejects the "absolute" authority of anything finite, it denounces the conservatism which sanctifies something decaying.

The churches either receive or suppress this prophetic spirit. If they suppress the prophetic spirit of self-criticism they are not compatible with the ideals of a free society. This is the condition for their compatibility.

Such criticism of course may lead to an emptying of the religious substance. The concreteness of religion may evaporate. If the priest disappears, the prophet loses the substance out of which he grows. Nevertheless, the prophet must be received, and if he is not received, then there is no compatibility between the free society and religion.

The second way in which I believe religion strengthens a free society is by forming the bearers of the free society. This happens in many ways. Religion does this directly by offering religious education. Religious education is initiation into the use of religious symbols, activities and communal life. Education which has nowhere to go, only a place to go from, is impossible. Religious education is concerned with bringing students into a religious group with concrete religious symbols; it does not merely mean teaching the history of religion. Religious education of this kind is the most basic way by which religion forms the bearers of a free society. It is also the most powerful way. But it is likewise full of danger. If it is effective, it produces absolutism. Yet, in spite of this danger, I would say that without its continuous effect, all the other ways of forming members of the free society by religion are ultimately impossible. So then, the question arises of how can the dangers of religious education be avoided. My answer is that at the right moment we must insert the critical element into every religious education. I believe there are three stages in the religious education of the young people:

First, we must give them the symbols of the tradition to which they belong. I missed that, and it was not good. I learned by experience. Without giving them first the symbols a vacuum is created, and when they grow up they accuse you for this vacuum in their lives.

The second stage is the moment in which the children ask questions, when the critical mind asserts itself. Here the great moment for the religious educator has come. Children must be shown that the religious symbols they have learned are not to be taken literally, but are symbols which answer their questions. If this is done, the critical period passes and the danger of a mere negative rebellion against religion will be avoided. The symbols will be understood as living answers to living questions.

The next way in which the members of a free society are shaped or formed by the religious or by religion is indirect. It is the way in which religion forms the substance of a culture. Every humanism is religiously founded and has religious substance. If you come from the outside, you can see immediately that in spite of the use of similar concepts in philosophy and forms in art and words in language, the spirit of different cultures is never the same; the spirit of a culture arises from the ultimate concerns of the culture. This is the indirect way in which religion forms all members of the social group, including those who emphatically insist they are wholly secular persons. Even then they cannot escape the fact that in the way they enjoy music or the theater or act morally towards others, there are principles at work and these principles were created out of someone's concern for the ultimate. Of course, the cultural forms must develop autonomously. They must develop according to their own inner laws, scientific laws, artistic laws, moral laws, political laws. The substance of them, however, that which gives them the title to be called principles, comes from somewhere else. That is given.

Now we can ask, are there special religions which have more kinship to a free society than others? Here I would answer on the basis of my limited knowledge of the non-Western religions with an unambiguous yes. Why? Because the free society presupposes affirmations which are based on the Old Testament and the traditions derived from the Old Testament, especially the Christian tradition. The basis for a free society in the sense that I defined it in the beginning is the affirmation of the personality of every individual as infinitely valuable in the sight of God.

There are two doctrines—symbolic doctrines of course as everything religious is symbolic—which alone make a free society possible. The one is the doctrine of creation and the other is the doctrine of history. Creation means that everything is good in so far as it *is,* not in so far as it is distorted but in so far as it is created. This means that every individual person has an infinite value, from the point of view of eternity. Only on this basis is the free society possible. Therefore, I don't believe that a free society can be derived from any religion unless the religion has been profoundly influenced by the Jewish tradition.

I am strengthened in this belief by the reports, repeated and repeated, that in India the most spiritual people, those who are the great saints, treat their servants most miserably. They do so because the concept of a *person* has no meaning for them. For them the human person is in a stage of development, the end of which is his return to the ultimate oneness, which certainly doesn't mean nothingness but a state beyond subject and object in which the personality, and therefore the community of love relationships, is impossible.

The other doctrine is that of the history of salvation—the history in which change is possible, change which is not only a circular movement, as in Greece and India, but the creation of something new. According to this doctrine every historical act in Western civilization, every liberation from servitude under false tyrannies, has an infinite meaning for the Kingdom of God. This gives to historical action the infinite seriousness which again I don't see in any comparable religion. This means that we in the West believe there is a possibility of transforming any given reality—of fighting against injustice, for instance.

I spoke about the affinity of the Western religion to the idea of a free society. An affinity between freedom and the religion of the West does not mean that the free society is an inevitable development. It might not come. Society, and we have seen this also, can be turned in the opposite direction, and something much worse than anything built on the foundations of the other religions might arise. The religious basis of Western culture can also be used to destroy the free society. We have experience with this in the modern totalitarian systems.

For my third point, religion judging the free society. Who are the judges? The judges are not necessarily church leaders or church assemblies or church goers; it may be that they are non-church people. But, whoever they are, they are grounded in the Jewish-Christian tradition. I re-

member the great Oxford Conference in 1937
where I served on the Committee on Socialism and
Communism and the relationship of these movements to the World Council of Churches. We
formulated a statement in which we said that it
might be that God speaks to the churches more
clearly through people who are enemies of the
churches than through the churches themselves.
This was a genuine prophetic feeling and was accepted at that time by the whole conference. It
was in the best spirit of Biblical prophetism.

What is the nature of the prophetic judgment?
Generally speaking, it must establish principles
and criticize abuses. But it must not make concrete
suggestions in the name of the church for transforming special forms of the social life into other
forms. This is better left to those who indirectly
or directly, as church members, are influenced by
the substance of religion; it is not done by the
churches when they speak as churches. This is an
experience I myself have had. In the flourishing
years of the religious socialist movement in Germany in the 1920's, we had ministers, laymen,
Jews and "pagans" of all forms—pagans in quotation marks because there are only Christian humanists in the Western world—in our movement.
We tried to provide a way for the Lutheran
churches and the Utopian socialist movement to
come together. We tried it by providing concepts
and symbols in which the unity between the two
could somehow be expressed. When young minis-

ters who belonged to our group went to their pulpits, I always told them not to preach religious socialism but to do two things: to preach the principles out of which religious socialism comes—principles of love expressed in the unity of justice and power—and to spell out what is against justice here and now, the making of men into cogs of a machine, into objects and *things*. (This was the main injustice of the time; and it is still in this country today.) Say this, I advised them, but don't preach religious socialism. Any ideas about socialism were mere political opinion, which should not be consecrated with the dignity of the holy.

Now, a final word about two principles of judgment. In a period of turbulence, both in individual lives and in the life of history, the church points to its symbols which show that despite restlessness and chaos there is an ultimate rest. This is the one message that the church always must preach. Today when I think of the generation in colleges and universities, this seems to be the most important message we can give them. In a disintegrating society, in the loss of symbols, in cynicism and the terrible feeling of emptiness, the church should show that there is another dimension to existence, there is still a source of fullness and of meaning and of truth. That is one thing the church can do for the free society.

The other thing is this. If the life of an individual person seems to have come to a standstill, then the church can stir up the forces of his being by making it uncomfortable for him to give up. This is the double function of the church in a free society. The destroyers of free society move in on chaos. So it was in Germany and in Russia. Through complacency freedom is slowly given up for the sake of conformity and the "good life." I don't believe that there is any force other than that force derived from the ultimate concern which can meet these two dangers.

NOTES ON CONTRIBUTORS

JOHN COURTNEY MURRAY is the editor of *Theological Studies*. He was ordained a priest of the Society of Jesus in 1933. Since that time he has taught at Woodstock College and at Yale. In 1957 he was appointed to the Fund for the Republic's Committee of Consultants on the Basic Issues.

REINHOLD NIEBUHR is vice-president of Union Theological Seminary. He is the author of many books, among them *The Nature and Destiny of Man, An Interpretation of Christian Ethics, Moral Man and Immoral Society* and *Beyond Tragedy*. He too is a member of the Committee of Consultants on the Basic Issues.

LEO PFEFFER, who is National Director of the American Jewish Congress' Commission on Law and Social Action, also serves as Associate General Counsel of the Congress. He is the author of *Church, State and Freedom* and *The Liberties of America*.

WILBER G. KATZ has been associated with the University of Chicago Law School since 1930, for several years as dean. Dr. Katz has written widely on the Church-State issue. He is a trustee of the Seabury Theological Seminary.

WILL HERBERG is professor of Judaic Studies at Drew University. He is the author of *Judaism and Modern Man, Protestant-Catholic-Jew* and numerous articles on religious and sociological questions.

JAMES HASTINGS NICHOLS is a member of the Federated Theological Faculty of the University of Chicago. Among his books are *Primer for Protestants* and *Democracy and the Churches*.

WALTER J. ONG joined the Society of Jesus in 1935 and was ordained in 1946. He is now professor of English in St. Louis University. Among his books are *Frontiers of American Catholicism* and *Ramus, Method and the Decay of Dialogue*.

STRINGFELLOW BARR, former president of St. John's College at Annapolis, is now teaching at Rutgers. His most recent book is *Purely Academic*, a satirical novel.

GUSTAVE WEIGEL is a leading Jesuit theologian. He served as dean of the theology faculty at the Catholic University of Chile until he was appointed to Woodstock College in 1949.

ABRAHAM JOSHUA HESCHEL received his rabbinical training in Europe. He is now a member of the faculty of the Jewish Theological Seminary of America. Rabbi Heschel is the author of *Man's Quest for God, God in Search of Man* and *Man Is Not Alone*.

PAUL TILLICH came to the United States from Germany in 1933 at the request of Union Theological Seminary. For almost a quarter of a century he taught at Union. In 1955 he was named professor of Systematic Theology at the Harvard Divinity School. His books have gained worldwide fame. Among them are *The Protestant Era, The Shaking of the Foundations, The Courage to Be* and *Systematic Theology*, his major work.

19762

261.7097.
C67

Date Due